Online Audio

JAZZ FIDDLE WIZARD

A PRACTICAL GUIDE TO JAZZ IMPROVISING FOR STRINGS

ONLINE AUDIO

1. A tuning note 440hz [:27]
2. G7 slow [1:56]
3. G7 fast [2:03]
4. Circle from D7, 8 measures each, slow [4:08]
5. Circle from D7, 8 measures each, fast [2:41]
6. My House, slow [4:04]
7. My House, fast [2:57]
8. Rose Room [4:38]
9. 2m-5-1's in G [2:02]
10. Good Lady [3:33]
11. Circle from D7, 2 measures each [1:49]
12. 2m-5-1's all keys [3:43]
13. Tune Down [3:10]
14. Minor 2ø-5-1m's in Em [2:06]
15. Minor 2ø-5-1m's all keys [3:24]
16. You Can't Appear Again [3:58]
17. Indiana (Back Home Again In), slow [3:47]
18. Indiana (Back Home Again In), fast [3:39]

by MARTIN NORGAARD

To Access the Online Audio Go To:
www.melbay.com/98379BCDEB

2 3 4 5 6 7 8 9 0

Visit us on the Web at http://www.melbay.com – E-mail us at email@melbay.com

FOREWORD

I received a total revelation in my early teens when I first heard Jean-Luc Ponty play acoustic violin in jazz (on the 1967 album *Sunday Walk*). He played (and still plays) with a power and forcefulness I had never imagined possible on the violin. He fit perfectly into the straight ahead jazz combo as if he played sax or trumpet. He improvised and projected his own style through the music, but at the same time played thoroughly within the jazz tradition. Later he changed to a more fusion oriented (and maybe even more personal) style, but that is another story.

After hearing *Sunday Walk* I became captivated with the violin in jazz. I explored the great players—Stuff Smith, Joe Venuti, Svend Asmussen, Stephane Grappelli, and others. I started listening to other jazz greats like Miles Davis, John Coltrane, Charlie Parker, and Thelonius Monk.

I tried to find an instruction book to get me started, but could not find one. Now, twenty years later, I have tried to write that book in the hope that others might find it useful. I called it *Jazz Fiddle Wizard* to set a goal. I keep working to reach the goal of the title, even though I know it will never be reached. Even the greatest players in jazz are always working on new ways to play that perfect solo. Enjoy the journey, because it will never be finished; hopefully this book will get you started in the right direction.

This book covers that first important step from written music to simple jazz—improvising. It contains both easy to understand theory and simple exercises. It also contains one solo transcription from the master jazz violinist, Stuff Smith, to introduce the concept of jazz rhythms. I have added an interactive element to the traditional workbook by committing myself to answer all questions concerning this book on my web site **jazzfiddlewizard.com**. The site also contains corrections and additions to this edition and features links to other jazz violin sites and resources.

Thank you for joining me in the quest to become a **Jazz Fiddle Wizard**.

Martin Norgaard, Nashville, December 1999.

ABOUT THE AUTHOR:

Martin Norgaard, Ph.D., is the author of the groundbreaking methods *Jazz Fiddle Wizard, Getting Into Gypsy Jazz Violin, Jazz Fiddle Wizard Junior, Jazz Viola Wizard Junior* and *Jazz Cello Wizard Junior Volumes 1* and 2 for Mel Bay Publications. He has also composed several orchestra pieces for FJH Music and is the co-author of the *Modern Violin Method* and the *Modern Viola Method* with Dr. Laurie Scott. Norgaard recently completed his doctoral studies in Music and Human Learning at The University of Texas at Austin. His dissertation *Descriptions of Improvisational Thinking by Artist-level Jazz Musicians* is a qualitative investigation of the cognitive processes underlying improvisation.

Norgaard taught jazz and commercial strings at Belmont University and Vanderbilt University in Nashville for six years, and was director of the Belmont Jazz String Quartet and Jazz String Septet, which were featured at IAJE 2001, MENC 2002 and ASTA 2003.

Norgaard holds bachelor's and master's degrees in jazz performance from William Paterson University, and Queens College in New York, where he studied with Rufus Reid, Hal Galper, Jimmy Heath and others.

Norgaard is a frequent clinician at state, national and international conventions such as Singapore International String Conference, ASTA, TMEA, SAA, OMEA, IMEA, GMEA, MENC, and IAJE, and has taught at summer workshops such as the IAJE Teacher Training Institute, the South Carolina Suzuki Institute, the Santa Fe Suzuki Institute, the Augusta Heritage Festival and Vanderbilt's International Fiddle School. Check out his web site at **JazzFiddleWizard.com.**

Other Martin Norgaard's titles for Mel Bay Publications include *French Tangos for Violin* (MB98223), and *Violin Wall Chart* (20276). He also transcribed Aubrey Haynie's Bluegrass fiddle record *Doin' My Time* (MB97178), Bonnie Rideout's Scottish fiddle record *Kindred Spirits* (MB98278) and *The Greatest Stars of Bluegrass Music* (fiddle edition) (MB97050) for Mel Bay.

INTRODUCTION

CONCEPT:

Jazz Fiddle Wizard is a workbook for string players who want to learn to improvise within the jazz tradition. It teaches the player how to improvise by using tunes and chord structures from the standard jazz repertoire. Though the book has some theory, it is not theory for the sake of theory. It introduces rhythms and scales that are quickly put to use. After completing lessons 1 through 25, the complete novice will be able to sit in at any blues or jazz jam session.

REQUIREMENTS:

Jazz Fiddle Wizard requires an open mind, an inquisitive spirit and a willingness to learn. It is presumed that the reader/player has a basic command of the instrument and elementary knowledge of music notation. The book has been "tested" on college students and other players of various technical ability and with backgrounds in classical and/or fiddle music. Put simply, IT WORKS!

FORMAT:

Jazz Fiddle Wizard is organized by tunes and lessons. It is recommended that all players—even those with prior experience improvising—start with lesson 1 and work their way through the book. It introduces concepts progressively and requires that the terms from the previous lessons are understood. Each lesson is organized in a theory and exercise section. One should try to make sense of the theory, then quickly move on to the exercises. The theory will make sense sooner or later. The main goal is to make music.

HELP:

Jazz Fiddle Wizard the book works in connection with jazzfiddlewizard the web site located at **http://www.jazzfiddlewizard.com**. This provides a unique interactive experience where the reader may pose questions directly to the author. The author will then respond either by personal e-mail or by posting answers to frequently asked questions. The site will also feature additional unpublished exercises and audio files and keep the reader up to date on other subjects relating to strings in jazz.

CONTENTS

ACKNOWLEDGMENTS

This book is dedicated to my mother, Jonna Hindsgaul, and jazz violinist Zbigniew Seifert. Both people inspired me to choose a life in music and education; both passed on before their time.

Of my own teachers, I would especially like to thank Leif Hindsgaul, David N. Baker, Rufus Reid, Jimmy Heath, and Svend Asmussen (who taught me one afternoon that "It don't mean a thing.........").

I would like to thank Jeff Kirk, Keith Ellis, Robert Gregg, Kris Elsberry, and Dean Cynthia Ann Curtis of the Belmont School of Music and Crystal D. Plohman and Dean Mark Wait of the Blair School of Music, Vanderbilt University.

Also many thanks to professor James C. Stamper at Belmont University's Department of Education for help with editing this book.

Thanks to Karen Pendley for patience and moral support during the writing process and to William A. Bay, president of Mel Bay Publications, for publishing the book.

A final thanks to all my students for being willing "guinea pigs" and providing invaluable feedback.

STUFF SMITH'S IMPROVISATION ON "KNOCK, KNOCK, WHO'S THERE?"

Stuff Smith and his Onyx Club Boys
New York, August 21, 1936.
transcription by Martin Norgaard

Suggested listening: Stuff Smith – The Complete 1936-1937 Sessions

LESSON 1:
RHYTHM

THEORY:

In jazz, the basic eighth note feel is the triplet swing eighth feel.

To learn about rhythm we refer to one of the masters of jazz violin, Stuff Smith. Even though history is not the focus of this book, some of the most famous players are used as examples. See "suggested listening" under each tune. I also encourage the reader to use the listings in the back to learn more about these performers.

Stuff Smith learned his phrasing from horn players—especially Louis Armstrong. He transferred basic jazz phrasing and rhythm to the violin in such a natural way that his playing is a great place to start for the beginning jazz string player. Tune 1 is a transcription of a solo from Stuff's 1936 recording of *Knock, Knock, Who's There?*

The whole solo is built on a triplet subdivision. That means that both regular eighth notes (see example 1) and all other rhythms (see examples 2 and 3) are played differently from the way they are written.

As seen in example 1, every off beat is delayed an amount equivalent to the last of three eighth note triplets. The first eighth note is therefore played longer than written, equivalent to the first two eighth notes of the triplet. As seen in examples 2 and 3, this also applies to all other eighth note rhythms. Though all this sounds complicated, it is just the swing groove or feel explained theoretically. The best way to learn this is to listen to and imitate the great jazz players.

EXERCISES:

1.) **Beat exercise 1 by hitting a table, using both hands.** The right hand beats the rhythm while the left beats triplets. By doing so, the rhythms are forced to fit in the right subdivision. Later try clapping the rhythms to a metronome or drum machine.

2.) **Imagine you are part of a marching band** and clap the rhythm in exercise 2. After clapping the written rhythms, make up your own, staying in the swing groove.

3ab.) **Play exercise 3a and 3b** as written on the open A string focusing only on rhythm. Play the eighth notes on the upper half of the bow. Even out the volume of the down and up strokes by putting a slight accent on the long eighth to counter the natural bow accent of the shorter stroke.

4.) **Clap the whole Stuff Smith solo** first very slowly then faster and faster using a metronome or drum machine. Listen to the actual solo if possible.

5.) **Play the Stuff Smith solo.** If you have the recording, copy his rhythm and phrasing as best you can. Remember there is nothing wrong with imitation, as long as you imitate many different players and only the best.

THEORY:

Example 1

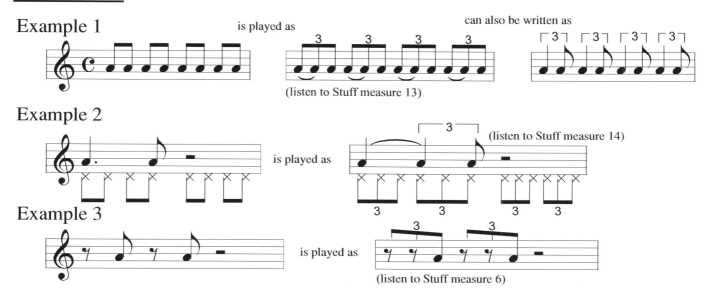

Example 2

Example 3

EXERCISES:

Exercise 1

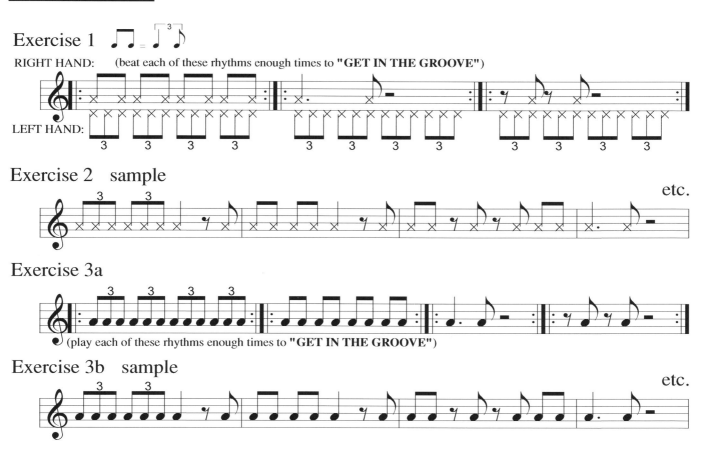

RIGHT HAND: (beat each of these rhythms enough times to **"GET IN THE GROOVE"**)

LEFT HAND:

Exercise 2   sample

etc.

Exercise 3a

(play each of these rhythms enough times to **"GET IN THE GROOVE"**)

Exercise 3b   sample

etc.

LESSON 2:
THE DOMINANT BEBOP SCALE

THEORY:

The basic premise of the dominant (mixolydian) bebop scale is: When playing swing eighth notes in jazz, try to place the chord notes on the beat. The bebop scale is constructed to accomplish this when playing eighth notes in scale motion.

The bebop scale that we will look at in this lesson is constructed to work over the dominant seven chord. We call it the dominant bebop scale. In this lesson we will focus on the G7 (see example 1). To probe our premise we construct the basic dominant scale and see if the notes on the beat are the notes of the G7 chord. As seen in example 2, everything is fine until we start the second octave where suddenly all the non-chord notes fall on the beat. To fix this, we add a chromatic note between f and g, creating a scale that has eight instead of seven notes (see example 3). We will later see that at any given point, even when changing direction, we still have chord notes on the beat (as in exercise 4). Also notice that the dominant scale in G functions as the five chord of C major and therefore has no accidentals in the key signature.

EXERCISES (CD tracks 2 and 3):

1.) **Play the G7 bebop** scale using the correct fingerings as shown in exercise 1. Notice the fingering around the chromatic steps are different going up and down. Also notice that the exercise remains in first position but utilizes the full register. This exercise should be done to track 2 or 3 on the accompanying CD. The notes in exercise 1 only represent the beginning of the exercise. The scale should be played continuously up and down until the end of the CD track. By doing this, the scale is practiced in two different variations with the scale starting on respectively the first and the third beat. It should be played on the upper half of the bow using smooth, light strokes. As with all other eighth notes in jazz, it should be played with a swing feel.

2.) **Jazz bowings**. Play the scale using the bowings shown in exercise 2. This bowing is the most commonly used bowing when playing swing eighth notes.

3.) **Mix the slurs with single strokes** as seen in exercise 3.

4.) **Change direction**. We now start adding an element of improvisation. We are still playing the scale without stops and in swing eighth. We start on the low G but can now change direction at any given point. Exercise 4 is only an example of this. Play your own version by changing direction when you want to. Use tracks 2 and 3 on the CD.

5.) **Change direction using jazz bowings**. Try combining exercise 4 with the bowings used in exercise 3. Remember we are still only playing the scale without stops.

THEORY:

Example 1   G7

Example 2   chord notes are on the beat   non-chord notes are on the beat

Example 3   all notes on the beat are now part of the G7 chord

EXERCISES:

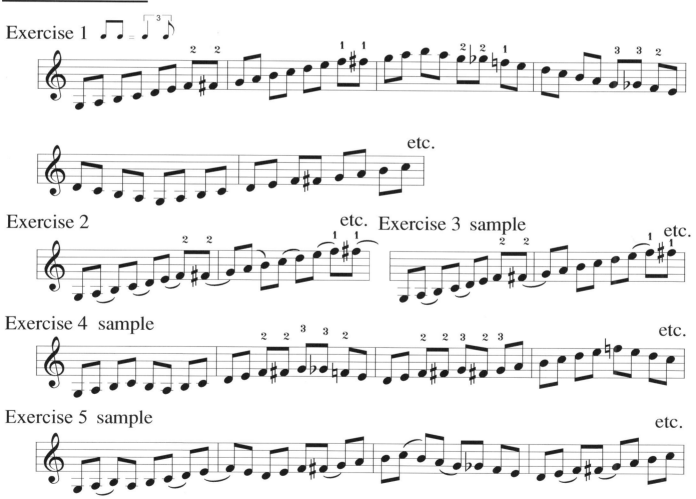

Exercise 1

Exercise 2   etc.   Exercise 3 sample   etc.

Exercise 4 sample   etc.

Exercise 5 sample   etc.

LESSON 3:
THE BEBOP SCALE WITH STOPS

THEORY:

To keep the chord notes on the beat we must start each eighth note lick either on a chord note on the beat or on a non-chord note off the beat.

If we want to keep the bebop scale premise that the basic chord notes of the dominant seven must be placed on the beat, we run into complications when we insert rests. When we start the eighth notes again we don't always want to start on the root or the first down beat. The first scenario is fairly simple: We want to start on the beat but not on the first beat of the measure and not on the root. As long as we start on a chord note we are fine (see example 2). The second scenario is when we start on the off-beat. Here we must start on a non-chord tone to end up on a chord tone on the following beat (see examples 3 and 4).

Keep in mind that we are still ONLY playing eighth notes and that even though we are moving slowly into the realm of improvising we are still only playing exercises and not "real" music.

EXERCISES (CD tracks 2 and 3):

1.) **Play all available chord tones** creating an arpeggio exercise that starts on the root, then goes to the top of the register in first position, then back down as seen in exercise 1. As in lesson 2, play the exercise continuously up and down to the CD tracks.

2.) **Play the G7 dominant bebop scale starting on a chord note other than the root, then stop and start again.** Try to visualize the available chord notes that you just played in exercise 1 and use these as starting notes. Experiment with changing direction and using jazz bowings. Exercise 2 sample is an example of how to do this. As with the following exercises make up your own versions while playing to CD tracks 2 and 3.

3.) **Start on a chord tone on the beat** but not on the first beat of the measure. See exercise 3 sample. This is a small rhythmic variation on exercise 2.

4.) **Start on the and of beat 4 on a non-chord tone.** Visualize a chord note then start one note below or above by counting yourself in ("1-2-3-4da, DA"). See exercise 4 sample.

5.) **Start on any off-beat on a non-chord tone.** As the exercises get a little more complicated they also start sounding like "the real thing." Jazz is a skill and just like any other discipline requires a certain amount of thinking. The great players don't think on stage only because they have practiced so much they don't have to think anymore, but just "feel." We'll get there! BE PATIENT!

THEORY:

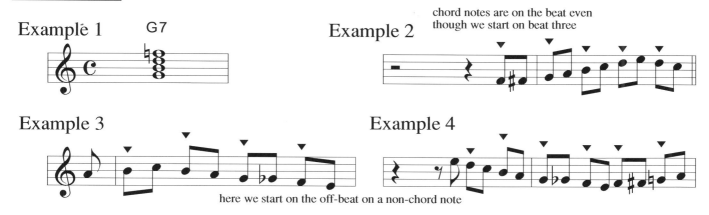

Example 1   G7

Example 2   chord notes are on the beat even though we start on beat three

Example 3

Example 4

here we start on the off-beat on a non-chord note

EXERCISES:

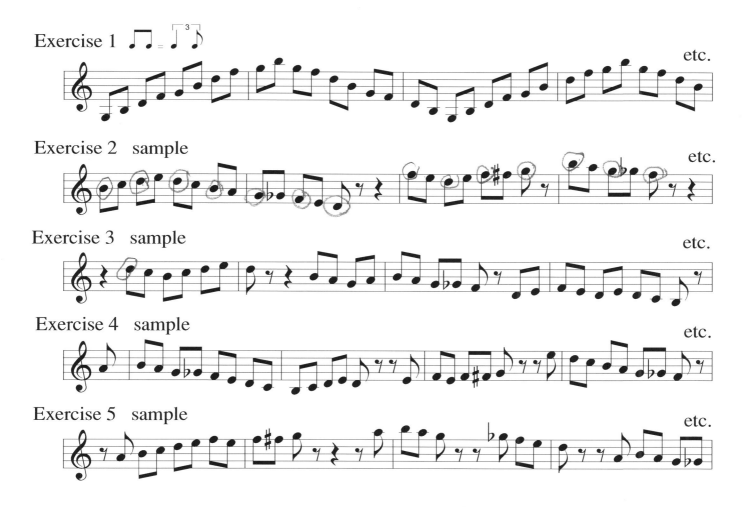

Exercise 1   etc.

Exercise 2   sample   etc.

Exercise 3   sample   etc.

Exercise 4   sample   etc.

Exercise 5   sample   etc.

LESSON 4:
TRANSPOSING THE BEBOP SCALE

THEORY:

The easiest way to play in many keys is by visualizing the fingering.

Imagine you are playing the mandolin. On the mandolin, there are only certain places you can put your fingers. The same is true on the violin, aside from slides and "blue notes." We therefore create the visual version of the fingering using finger patterns. On the next page are the finger patterns for D7, G7, C7, and F7 dominant bebop scales (C7 is unfinished but more about that later). Notice that the circle that represents each finger is between the lines representing our imaginary frets. Also notice that the circle fills out all the space between the imaginary frets.

● : Represents the finger position of the root (D in the D7 bebop scale).

◉ : Represents chord tones other than the root (F♯, A, and C in the D7 bebop scale).

○ : Represents regular scale notes that are non-chord tones (E, G, and B in D7).

⬚ : Represents the extra note we inserted into the mixolydian scale to make it a bebop scale. Going up, this note is usually played with the finger below moving up to this position. Going down, it is usually the finger above that moves down. In D7 it is the C♯ (or D♭) on the A string played either with a 2nd finger ascending or 3rd finger descending. Notice that we always play the C♯ (or D♭) on the G string in this key with the low 4th, always utilizing the open D whether ascending or descending.

(○) : A large parenthesis around certain 4th fingers means use of the 4th on that string is optional.

✗ : Means the open string is not in the scale. This symbol is first used in lesson 10.

EXERCISES:

1.) **Finish the C7 dominant bebop scale finger pattern** using the principles from above. Then check it by playing it and by looking at the notated scale.

2.) **Finish writing out the F7 dominant bebop scale** using regular notation in the provided space. Notice that all the scale exercises are equivalent to exercise 1 from lesson 2. They always start on the root. Then they go to the highest note within the scale in first position then to the lowest note possible then back up to (or past) the root.

THEORY:

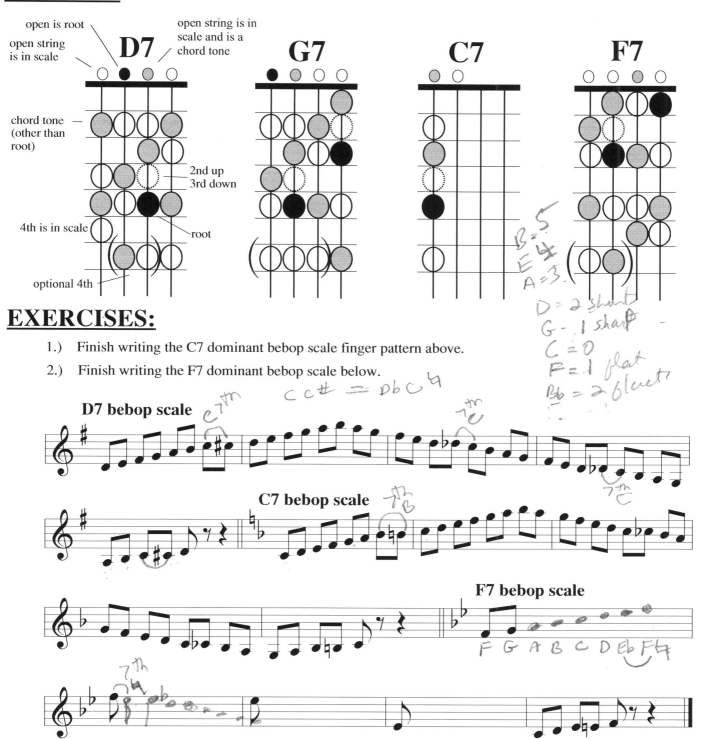

EXERCISES:

1.) Finish writing the C7 dominant bebop scale finger pattern above.

2.) Finish writing the F7 dominant bebop scale below.

LESSON 5:
THE BEBOP SCALE IN D, G, C, AND F

THEORY:

Transpose all the exercises from lessons 2 and 3 to D, C, and F using the correct fingerings. Ascending, the extra step is usually played with a finger moving up. Descending, it is normally played with a finger moving down.

Using the practice CD tracks 4 and 5, do all the exercises from lessons 2 and 3 in the new keys. The CD plays each key for eight measures through all keys. For now, stop the CD after F7 and start it again for the following exercise. First run the scales up and down, then change direction, then play with stops and starts on and off the beat.

The fingerings are different going up and down for two reasons. First, they are designed to use the space between the on and off beats that are caused by the swing feel, to move the sliding finger without letting the listener hearing the slide. Secondly, they fit the jazz bowings, so two notes played with the same finger are never slurred. To clearly define the chromatics with good intonation, the open strings should be used as much as possible.

EXERCISES (CD tracks 4 and 5, first 4 keys):

1.) **Play each scale starting on the root** all the way to the top of first position, then to the lowest note, then back up, etc., for eight measures. Leave a little space between each key. Be very careful to use the correct fingerings—they are different going up and down. The exercise is written exclusively with accidentals instead of changing key signatures for easy reading. Ascending notes are generally written as sharps, descending as flats, thereby matching the correct fingering.

2.) **Play exercise 1 again using jazz slurs.**

3.) **Play exercise 1 once more with a combination of single strokes and jazz slurs.**

4.) **Change direction.** Play the scales up and down but change direction when you choose. The written exercise 4 sample is only an example of this. Make your own version. Remember, we still cannot skip notes. Mix in jazz bowings.

5.) **Play the chord notes of the dominant 7 chord in the four keys** again, starting on the root, then all the way up, then all the way down, then back up, etc.

6.) **Start each key on a chord note on the beat** other than the root. Then stop and start again on another chord note. Again the written music is only a sample.

7.) **Start each key on a non-chord note off the beat**. Then stop and start again. Take long pauses to think. You have eight measures for each key. **IMPROVISE!!!!**

EXERCISES:

Exercise 3   sample

etc.

Exercise 4   sample

18

Exercise 5

Exercise 6 & 7 sample

This page has been left blank
to avoid awkward page turns.

MY HOUSE

Up tempo

Martin Norgaard

Suggested listening: "Pent-up House," Various Artists - Violin Summit

LESSON 6:
TUNE ANALYSIS

THEORY:

All standard jazz tunes can be analyzed using a simple number system. The dominant bebop scale works on any dominant 7th chord and on its related 2 minor if it appears right before the 5.

In order to figure out where we can use the bebop scale on a jazz tune we must first analyze the chords. We assign a number to each scale step with the root being number one. In this lesson we use *My House* as an example for analysis. *My House* uses the same chord progression for improvising as the Sonny Rollins tune *Pent-up House*.

We are in the key of G major. See example 1 for the numbers in G major. In example 2, all the diatonic chords of G major are listed. Diatonic means that all notes in the chords are part of the G major scale. Other books go into great detail concerning these principles (e.g., Robert Ottman's book listed in the bibliography). That is not the focus of this book, so we continue. For our purpose we only need to analyze three of the seven diatonic chords. Notice that the only diatonic dominant 7th chord is on the 5th step. We therefore refer to it as a "5" chord. On the 2nd step is a minor 7th chord. We are about to discover that in nearly all standard jazz tunes we find lots of 2m-5-1's. This is the jazz version of the classical cadence (subdominant-dominant-tonic).

Take a look at example 3. Here, all the chords of *My House* are analyzed in numbers. Notice that in the third line there are two 5 chords that are not D7 (the 5 chord in G major). Therefore we know that the tune modulates even though it never reaches the new 1 chords. The analysis is therefore first done from C major since G7 is the five of C, then from B♭ major because F7 is the 5 of B♭. The 2m-5's never resolve.

We are now ready to start applying the bebop scales. First, please accept this simple rule about the scale—it can be used both on the 5 chords and their related 2m's. Therefore we can use the D7 bebop scale in the first 2 measures. We then change to a regular G major scale in measures 3 and 4. The same in the next line. In line three, use G7 bebop on the first two measures, then switch to the F7 bebop.

As we analyze more tunes these principles will become clearer and seem much easier.

THEORY:

MY HOUSE
(chord analysis)

LESSON 7:
USING THE BEBOP SCALE

THEORY:

We construct a bebop scale line on the 2m and 5, then resolve on the 1 chord.

Using the bebop scale on *My House* is simply applying the rules we practiced in lessons 2 through 5, except we have to resolve the line. In this tune, the 2m-5 is resolved to 1 in lines 1, 2, and 4, as we saw in lesson 6. After playing the bebop scale on the 2m-5, we have to construct a simple figure that ends the eighth note line in a logical manner. The easiest way to do this is by playing a simple figure around the 1 major seven chord (see examples 1 and 2). In example 2, a blues passing tone (Bb) is added for color. Use CD tracks 6 and 7 to practice the following exercises.

EXERCISES (CD tracks 6 and 7):

1.) **Play the dominant bebop scales** starting on the root on the first beat, corresponding to our scale analysis from lesson 6. Play up the scale until you reach the top note in first position, then back down to the 2m-5 changes. In lines 1, 2, and 4, resolve to a simple figure on the 1 chord. In line 3 go straight to the following bebop scale. Before each scale change we may "cut out" the last eighth note by turning the last note in the 2m-5 into a quarter note. In this exercise only the bars containing the 1 chord where we play a REGULAR G MAJOR SCALE (measures 3, 4, 7, 8, 15, and 16) are improvised.

2.) **Start on the root, but change direction**. We now end up in different places when reaching the 1 chord (lines 1, 2, and 4) or the next bebop scale (line 3). We are still only playing scales over the 2m-5's in a continuous line of eighth notes. Remember to use the different fingerings going up and down. Exercises 2 to 6 develop the lines in the measures containing bebop scales. On Gmaj7 play a simple melody as in exercise 1.

3.) **Start on a chord note other than the root,** but still on the first beat. Remember, we are ignoring the 2 minor chords, so consider both measures 1 and 2 a D7. The chord notes are D, F♯, A, and C.

4.) **Start on any chord note on the beat. This time avoid starting on the first beat**.

5.) **Start on the off-beat on any non-chord tone** within the bebop scale measures.

6.) **Experiment with start and stops** within the bebop scale measures.

Remember this book is all about improvising WITHIN a framework of rules. These rules will become less and less stringent as we go along. BE PATIENT!!!!

THEORY:

Example 1   Example 2

EXERCISES ON "MY HOUSE":

Please Remember: You won't learn to improvise if you only play the following samples as written. First play the sample, then improvise to the CD track using the guidelines outlined for each exercise on the previous page.

Exercise 1 sample

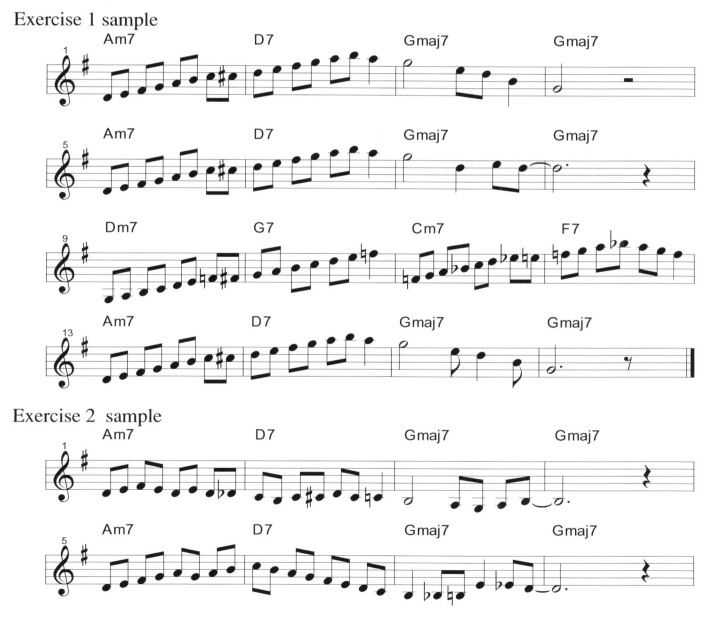

Exercise 2 sample

Exercise 3 sample

Exercise 4 sample

Exercise 5 sample

Exercise 6 sample

LESSON 8:
RHYTHM, PART 2

THEORY:

The key to melodic freedom is RHYTHM.

Look once again at the Stuff Smith solo in the beginning of the book. He doesn't always follow the chords exactly. Look at the next to last measure where he starts playing on the last E♭ major chord two beats early. It works because he plays with exact super swinging rhythms. As we saw in lesson 1, the whole solo makes sense simply clapped.

In the following exercises, we practice this on the tune from lesson 6, *My House*, simply by inserting rhythms in the framework from lesson 7. We will try to use the scales from lesson 6 and 7 but the main focus in this lesson is rhythm—we can use rhythms ANYWHERE. When we play a strong rhythm we can play nearly ANYTHING!

Examples 1, 2, 3, 4, and 5 are rhythms taken from the Stuff Smith solo.

EXERCISES (CD tracks 6 and 7):

1.) **Play each of the rhythms from examples 1-5** on an open string using a metronome, drum machine or the *My House* track. Use a strong triplet swing feel, as we practiced in lesson 1. If possible listen to the Stuff Smith solo to check accuracy and phrasing.

2.) **Play a solo to *My House*** to track 6 or 7 using one of the rhythms from above. You can use any pitch to create small melodies. This exercise is not included on the next page.

3.) **Play a solo to *My House* using all of the rhythms from above.** The written exercise is only one way to do this. Remember, when playing a rhythm you are free to play any pitch.

4.) **Play bebop scales on all the 2m-5's, then resolve the eighth note line with a strong rhythm on the Gmaj7.** You can use any of the exercises from lesson 7; just end each bebop scale lick with a Stuff Smith rhythm (examples 1-5) on the Gmaj7. In lesson 7 we just played a simple melody on the Gmaj7 focusing mainly on the bebop scales. This exercise is not included on the next page.

5.) **Play rhythms anywhere you like** but still try and mix in some bebop scale lines.

THEORY:

Example 1 Stuff measure 2:

Example 2 Stuff measure 5 & 6:

Example 3 Stuff measure 11:

Example 4 Stuff m. 21:

Example 5 Stuff measure 4 & 5:

EXERCISES:

Exercise 3 Sample

Exercise 5 Sample

This page has been left blank
to avoid awkward page turns.

ROSE ROOM

Williams/Hickman
arr. M. Norgaard

Suggested listening: Django Reinhardt & Stephane Grappelli

LESSON 9:

REVIEW AND *ROSE ROOM*

THEORY:

In the previous 8 lessons we have learned jazz rhythm, how to place the chord notes on the beat, and simple tune analysis.

Let us review what the bebop scale is all about. The rules force us to place the chord notes from the dominant seven chord on the beat. Therefore when we improvise following these rules, we play "inside" the chord and firmly within the jazz tradition. Similarly, by using strong rhythm, we play within the jazz tradition.

In this lesson we combine it all and use what we learned to improvise on an old standard called *Rose Room*. As we see in the analysis on the next page, most of the 2 chords and the following 5's are dominants (measures 1, 13, 14, 17, and 29). That gives us plenty of places to use the bebop scale. Why are nearly all the 2 chords now dominants instead of 2 minors? Remember that the analysis is always after the fact. The composers do what they want to. The analysis gives us a reference that helps us connect and remember the chord patterns we improvise over, even if we have to remember that a particular tune DOES NOT follow certain rules.

In addition, we find a couple of 4 minors going to ♭7 dominant chords (measures 9-10 and 25-26). This is an example of a 2m-5 that resolves but not to the expected 1 chord. For now just accept this and try to resolve the bebop scale logically.

EXERCISES (CD track 8):

1.)   Play the bebop scale on all the 2-5's starting on the root and resolve to a rhythm. We play the corresponding bebop scale on the dominant 2's but ignore the minor 2's. See the scale analysis on the next page. Examples are not written for exercises 1-3.

2.)   Play the bebop scale on all the 2-5's starting on the beat on a chord note other than the root and resolve to a rhythm.

3.)   Play the bebop scale on all the 2-5's starting on an off-beat on a non-chord tone and resolve to a rhythm.

4.)   Mix in bebop scales with rhythms anywhere. See written solo example. This solo is a fairly free interpretation of our bebop scale and rhythm rules. It contains a couple of chromatic passing tones (measures 1, 3, 17, 22, 29, and 30; see lesson 12) as well as some bebop scale phrases placed "wrong" (measures 14 and 18). This is done to show that, just as with chord analysis, the rules are meant to be broken when it makes sense melodically.

ROSE ROOM
(chord analysis)

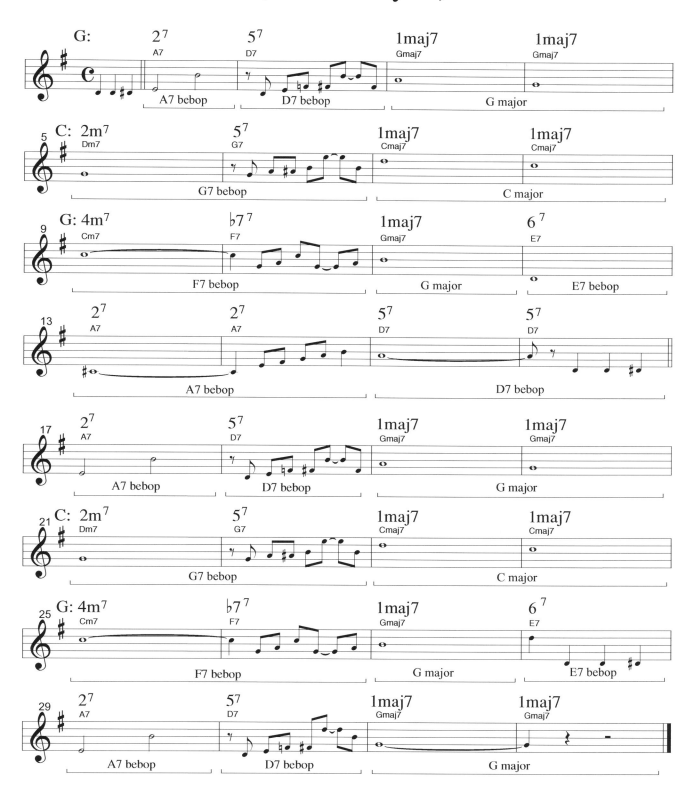

ROSE ROOM
(Solo example)

This page has been left blank
to avoid awkward page turns.

LESSON 10:
THE BEBOP SCALE IN B♭, E♭, A♭, AND D♭

THEORY:

We use the principles from lessons 4 and 5 to transpose the bebop scale to B♭, E♭, A♭, and D♭.

The new keys are not harder to play except there aren't as many open strings available. The principle of the extra step, of an ascending line being played with a finger sliding up, and a descending line being played with a finger sliding down, are still the same. This lesson is essentially lessons 4 and 5 in one lesson, but in new keys. For explanation of the finger patterns, see lesson 4. For full length samples of the exercises, see lesson 5.

Use CD tracks 4 and 5, but stop after D♭. Review D, G, C, and F then make sure you are just as comfortable when the circle of fifth continues into B♭, E♭, A♭, and D♭.

EXERCISES (CD tracks 4 and 5, first 8 keys):

1.) **Play each scale starting on the root** all the way to the top of first position, then to the lowest note, then back up, etc., for eight measures. When using tracks 4 and 5 you may play the more advanced exercises including starts and stops in the easier keys. Then when the track goes into the new keys switch back to this simple exercise.

2.) **Play exercise 1 again using jazz slurs.** Samples are not written for exercises 2-7. Please refer to the samples in lesson 5 and transpose to the new keys.

3.) **Play exercise 1 once more with a combination of single strokes and jazz slurs.**

4.) **Change direction.** Play the scales up and down, changing direction when you want. Remember we still cannot skip notes. Mix in jazz bowings.

5.) **Play the chord notes of the dominant 7 chord in the eight keys** again, starting on the root, then all the way up, then all the way down, then back up, etc.

6.) **Start each key on a chord note on the beat** other than the root. Then stop and start again on another chord note.

7.) **Start each key on a non-chord note off the beat.** Then stop and start again. Take long pauses to think. You have eight measures for each key. IMPROVISE!!!!

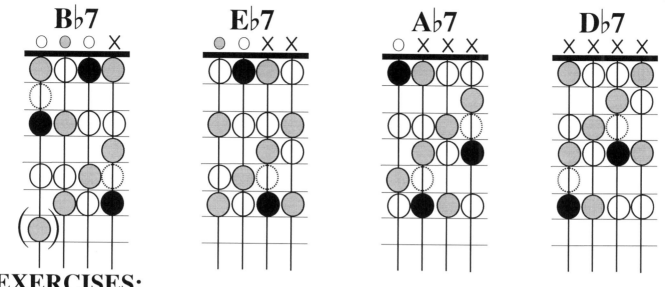

EXERCISES:

Exercise 1

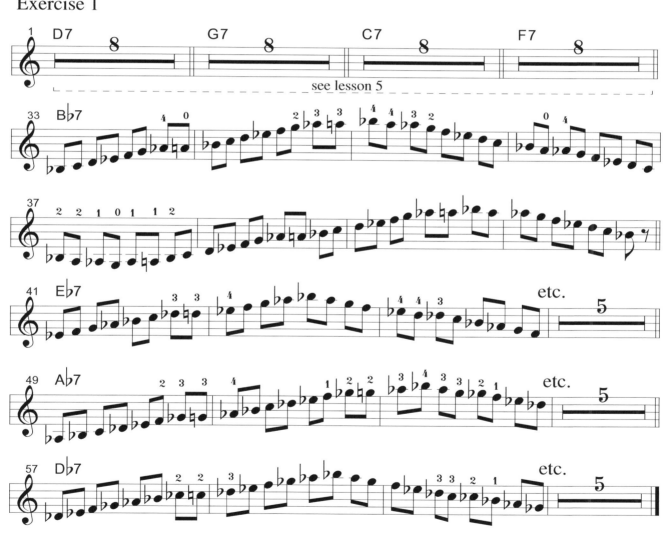

LESSON 11:
INNER MELODIES

THEORY:

To connect changing chords, we improvise over a melody that spells out the particular chord change. The concept of the inner melody is referred to as "voice leading" by players of chordal instruments such as piano and guitar. The last note of the melody is referred to as the "target note."

Although we have played over changing chords, we have so far looked at each chord as a separate entity. Each chord was analyzed as corresponding to a particular scale. In this lesson we will focus on connecting the chords.

Once again we will use tracks 4 and 5 from the CD. We know each of the bebop scales—D, G, C, F, B♭, E♭, A♭, and D♭—from the previous lessons. In this lesson we will focus on the measures where the exercises change keys and learn how to smoothly improvise over those changes.

Example 1 shows the first chord change between D7 and G7. There are various possible inner melodies that outline this change. The inner melody we will focus on in this lesson is the ♭7 of the first chord going chromatically down and becoming the 3 of the next chord. Example 2 shows the inner melodies only. The last note is referred to as the target note.

Once again, if this doesn't make much sense theoretically skip right to the exercises below. They are very easy!!

EXERCISES (CD tracks 4 and 5, first 8 keys):

1.) **Play only the inner melody.** For each key find the ♭7 note and play it in measure 8 of each key and resolve it to the 3rd of the next key. Then count 6 empty measures and play the ♭7 of this key and resolve to the 3rd of the next key and so on.

2.) **Repeat exercise 1 but insert bebop scale runs** where we counted empty measures in the previous exercise. Keep the bebop scale figures simple with no rhythms so you can count measures. Remember, we are focusing on the key changes, not the scales.

3.) **Insert rhythms in the measures around the key changes.** Use the inner melody to create a new figure using rhythms. GO BACK TO COUNTING EMPTY MEASURES BETWEEN KEY CHANGES. The written exercise is only one way to do this. IMPROVISE!!!

4.) **Use rhythms AND play bebop scale lines.** Combine exercises 2 and 3. We are now improvising in many keys AND connecting the keys logically. This exercise is not written out.

THEORY:

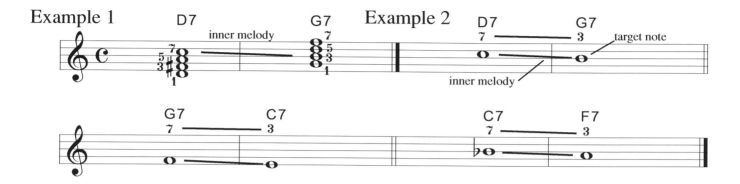

EXERCISES:

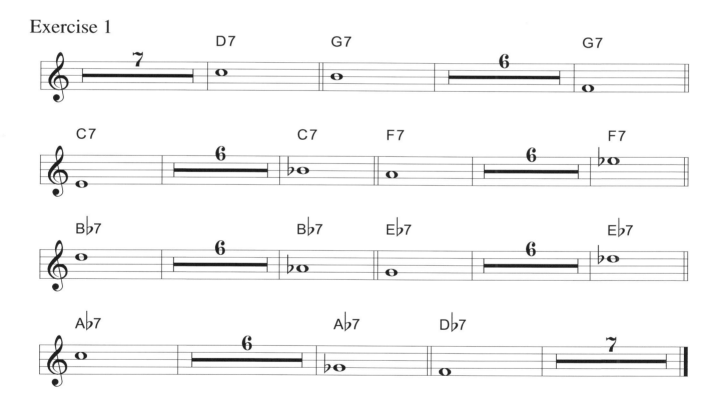

Exercise 2 sample

Exercise 3 sample

LESSON 12:
2m-5-1 ARPEGGIOS

THEORY:

The 2m-5-1 is the most common progression in jazz. Even though the 2m and the 5 chord are most often written as 7th chords one can play arpeggios all the way up to the 13th.

In the next two lessons we will expand the scale and rhythm approach from previous lessons to include arpeggios. We use the major 2m-5-1 because by learning to play on a 2m-5-1 in all keys you automatically learn to navigate through most tunes. The three chords of the 2m-5-1 represent three different types of chords roughly equivalent to the cadence in classical theory: The 2m chord functions as the subdominant, the 5 chord as the dominant and the 1 chord as the tonic.

In this lesson it is important to realize that we deal with two different sets of numbers. 2m-5-1 refers to the root of each chord's number on the 1 chord's major scale. We call those **SCALE STEP NUMBERS** (see examples 1 and 3).

The second set of numbers (the 7 of the D7) refers to the extensions in relation to the root of each chord. We call those **EXTENSION NUMBERS** (see examples 2 and 3).

Example 3 shows the chords of a 2m-5-1 in G major. The regular 7th chords are written normally and the implied upper extensions (9, 11, and 13) are marked in squares. On the 1 chord the 11th should be avoided and the 13th is looked upon as the 6th.

EXERCISES (CD track 9):

1.) **Play the basic chords as arpeggios, but without using upper extensions**. Start on the root, then arpeggiate the chord by playing the root, third, fifth, and seventh. Repeat the same notes in the next octave. When we reach the top of our register in first position go back down. Play this and the following exercises repeatedly, using track 9 on the CD.

2.) **Play the chords as arpeggios but in different inversions**. In other words, play the same notes as in exercise 1 but don't start on the roots.

3.) **Combine exercises 1 and 2 with a simple bebop scale lick**. The written exercise is only one way to do this. Make up your own.

4.) **Play arpeggios using the upper extensions**. Start on the root and arpeggiate the chord, playing the root, 3rd, 5th, 7th, 9th, 11th, and 13th on Am7 and D7. On Gmaj7, we play the root, 3rd, 5th, 6th, major 7th, and 9th.

5.) **Play arpeggios including upper extensions in different inversions**. Start on a note other than the root and arpeggiate up to the 13th (or 9th on Gmaj7), then change direction and go back down. PLEASE NOTICE WE STILL ALWAYS PLAY IN THIRDS WITH NO OTHER SKIPS (except when we play the 6th on Gmaj7).

THEORY:

Example 1

Example 2

Example 3

EXERCISES:

Exercise 1

Exercise 2 sample

Exercise 3 sample

Exercise 4

Exercise 5 sample

LESSON 13:
ARPEGGIO SHAPES

THEORY:

Arpeggio shapes are a way of looking at arpeggios that makes it easier to incorporate upper extensions in improvised lines.

Improvisation using arpeggios is a completely different concept than using the bebop scale. The bebop scale was built on the assumption that the upper extensions of the chord, 9, 11, and 13, were non-chord tones. In this lesson we will learn how to use the extensions when improvising using arpeggios.

In lesson 12, exercise 4 we played the chords of the 2m and 5 in G from the root all the way up to the 13th. That means we actually played all the notes of the G major scale but structured them so it sounded like an Am13 or G13. When playing arpeggios using the upper extensions we don't want to be forced to outline the full chord. But, if we don't play the full chord, how do we make sure it still sounds like we are playing the right chords? The answer is, we use certain shapes similar to chord voicings that specifically outline the most interesting notes of the chord. This way we can outline a D13 without having to play all 7 notes.

There are two basic ways of using arpeggio shapes. The CONSTANT SHAPES progression uses the same configuration on each chord (see example 1). The CHANGING SHAPES progression changes chord configuration but uses as many common tones between chords as possible (see example 2).

Example 3 lists a couple of other great sounding shapes on the Am7-D7-Gmaj7 progression. Notice that many of the shapes look like completely different chords – e.g., the first chord in example 3c looks like a Cmaj7 though it actually is a Am9 because of the bass note dictated by the chord symbol above.

Arpeggios are enormously complex. Though this lesson by no means covers all possible ways of improvising using arpeggios, it should get you going on the right track.

EXERCISES (CD track 9):

1.)   Arpeggiate any of the shapes in examples 1 to 3. The sample uses example 3c. Play all the exercises to track 9 on the CD.

2.)   Arpeggiate the shapes using more than one octave. Change direction when you please. The sample uses example 2 ascending on the Am7, then descending on the D7. Try this with another shape.

3.)   Arpeggiate a shape but change direction and add skips. The sample uses the shapes from example 3d.

4.)   Use shapes from different examples and add bebop scales and rhythms. The most effective way to use arpeggios is in combination with other approaches like rhythms or bebop scales. We will explore this further in lesson 14 and when we use arpeggios while improvising on tunes.

THEORY:

Example 1

Constant shapes: 9th, 3rd, 5th & 7th

Example 2

Changing shapes: 9th, 3rd, 5th & 7th

Example 3

Constant shapes | Changing shapes

Changing shapes | Changing shapes | Changing shapes
(even though the notes stay the same from Am7 to D7 it is a "Changing Shape" because the notes represent different extensions)

EXERCISES:

Exercise 1 sample

Exercise 2 sample

Exercise 3 sample

Exercise 4 sample

LESSON 14:
2m-5-1 SCALES AND MELODIES

THEORY :

The basic scales of the 2m and the 5 have the same notes as the 1 major.

In this lesson we will explore the scale options further and add the inner melodies from lesson 11 to the 2m-5-1. Example 1 shows the ♭7-3 connection between the 5 and the 1 chord. Notice the 7th of the D7—the note C, also represents the 3rd of the 2m chord so the note works on both the 2m and the 5.

We have two options on the 2m chord. We can either ignore it and start the bebop scale early (see lesson 6) or look at it as a separate chord and scale. The theory behind the second option is that we simply stay within the G major scale but emphasize the basic A minor chord (not the upper extensions). A good way to emphasize the chord notes is by placing them on the beat. That means we actually improvise on the 2nd step of the major scale (also referred to as the dorian minor). Starting the major scale from the 5th step is referred to as a mixolydian. Again just stay within G major but emphasize the basic D7 chord (or simply play D7 bebop scale). See example 2.

The following exercises first use the basic scales, then all the elements from the previous lessons are added—bebop scales (lessons 2-5, 7, and 10), rhythms (lessons 1 and 8), inner melodies (lesson 11), and arpeggios (lessons 12 and 13). As in the previous two lessons, use track 9 on the CD.

EXERCISES (CD track 9):

1.) **Play the basic scales (not bebop scales) ascending in eighth notes starting on the roots**.

2.) **Play the basic scales on Am and G but bebop on the D7.** This time start on a chord note other than the root. Change direction. Stay with all eighth notes. The written exercises are only samples. IMPROVISE!

3.) **Ignore the 2m and play D7 bebop scale with stops on the first two measures**. End the phrase with a good rhythm on the Gmaj7 (see lessons 7 and 8).

4.) **Add the inner melody**. Play D7 bebop scale on the first two measures but end on a C. Then resolve the C to a B and finish the phrase melodically.

5.) **Play arpeggios on the Am, then go into D7 bebop landing on a C. Resolve to B and play a melodic rhythm**. They say jazz stimulates the mind!

6.) **MIX IT ALL UP AND MAKE IT YOUR OWN**. If it helps, write out more 2m-5-1 licks using the principles from the previous exercises.

THEORY:

Example 1

Example 2

EXERCISES:

Exercise 1

Exercise 2 sample

Exercise 3 sample

Exercise 4 sample

Exercise 5 sample

Exercise 6 sample

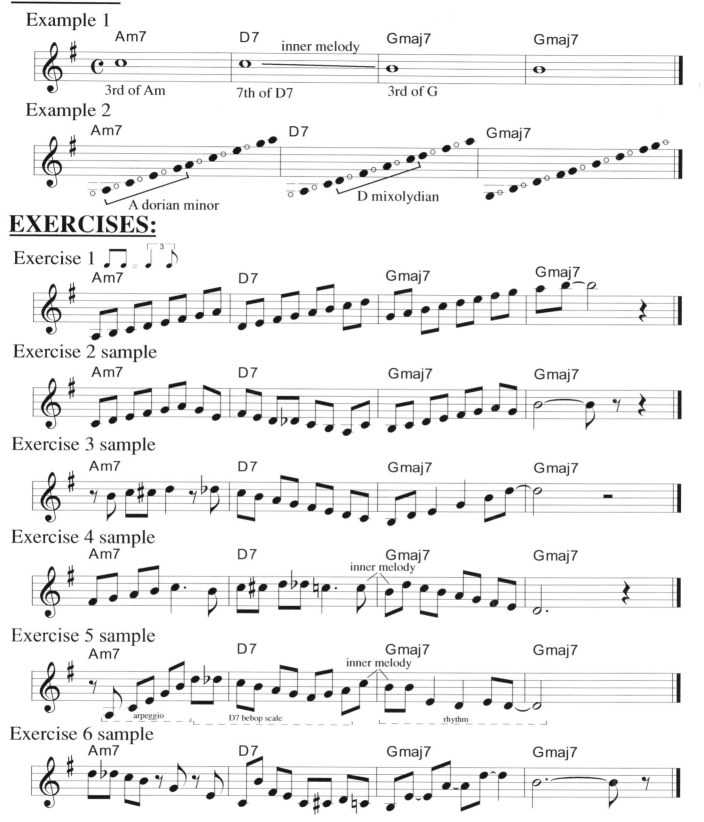

This page has been left blank
to avoid awkward page turns.

GOOD LADY

Medium up

Martin Norgaard

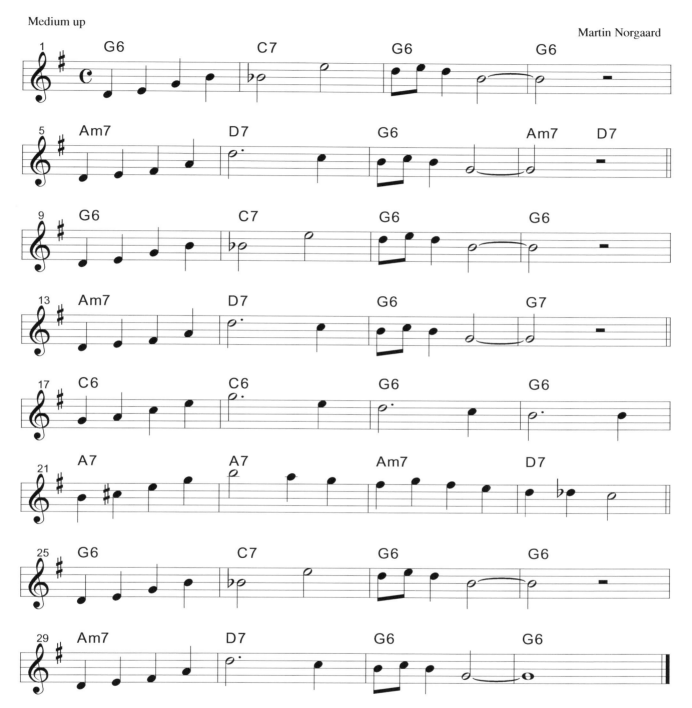

Suggested listening: "Oh, Lady Be Good!" Svend Asmussen - Musical Miracle

LESSON 15:

CHORD CATEGORIES AND *GOOD LADY*

THEORY:

Most chords belong to either the 2m, 5, or 1 chord family. Many tunes use the AABA form.

In this lesson we will analyze and improvise over *Good Lady*, using everything we have learned so far. The chords in *Good Lady* are similar to the chords in the classic swing tune *Oh, Lady Be Good!* Example 2 shows the analysis of *Good Lady*. Notice that the chords in measures 1-8 are nearly identical to the chords of measures 9-16 and 25-32. We call those sections the A sections. Measures 17-24 are referred to as the B section. When we put it all together, we get AABA, which is a common form used in standard jazz tunes. To improvise effectively over a tune, the chords must be memorized and knowing the form of the tune makes that much easier.

In lessons 6 and 12 we saw that nearly all jazz chords can be divided into three categories, each representing a chord in the 2m-5-1. In lesson 12 we saw that you can arpeggiate up to the 13th of the Am even though the chart only lists Am7. That is because Am7, Am9, Am11, and Am13 are all in the 2m category. Similarly D7, D9, D11, and D13 are all in the 5 chord category. The 1 chord category includes Gmaj7, G6, and G6$^{(add9)}$. See example 1 on the opposite page and examples 2 and 3 in lesson 12. Any chord can usually be substituted for any other chord in the same category. This means that on all the G6 and C6 chords in this tune we can simply play the regular G major or C major scales just as we did on the Gmaj7 chord in all the previous lessons. Notice that this tune contains two types of C chords: C7 in measures 2, 10, and 26 is a 5 chord (even though it is the 4 of G), so we can play C bebop scale or C13 arpeggios; C6 in measures 17 and 18 is a 1 chord so we play C major or C6, Cmaj7, or C6$^{(add9)}$ arpeggios.

EXERCISES (CD track 10):

1.) **Play scales ascending on each chord, starting on the root.** Only the beginning of each exercise is written out. Continue playing the same exercise until the end of track 10 on the practice CD.

2.) **Play scales but change direction without starting on the roots.** Remember the bebop scales rules on all the dominant seven chords.

3.) **Play scales and rhythms.**

4.) **Play scales and rhythms and use the ♭7-3 inner melody on all 2m-5-1's.**

5.) **Play every chord as a simple arpeggio starting on the root.**

6.) **Play arpeggios in different inversions.**

7.) **Improvise combining all of the above.** See solo example.

THEORY:

Example 1

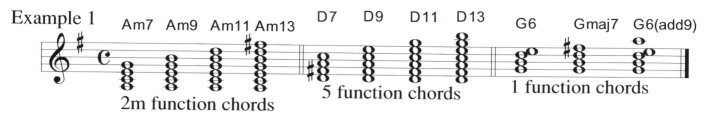

2m function chords   5 function chords   1 function chords

GOOD LADY
(Chord analysis)

Example 2

Exercise 1

Exercise 2 sample

Exercise 3 sample

Exercise 4 sample

Exercise 5 sample

Exercise 6 sample

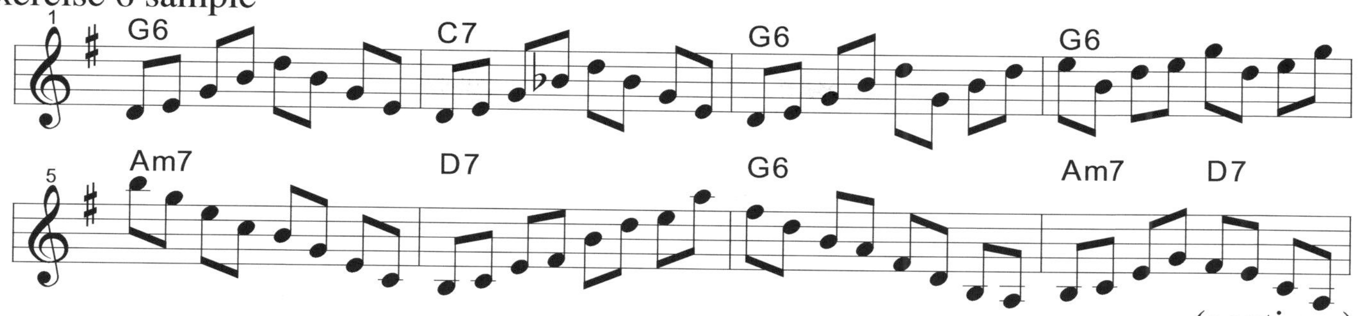

(continue)

GOOD LADY
(Solo example)

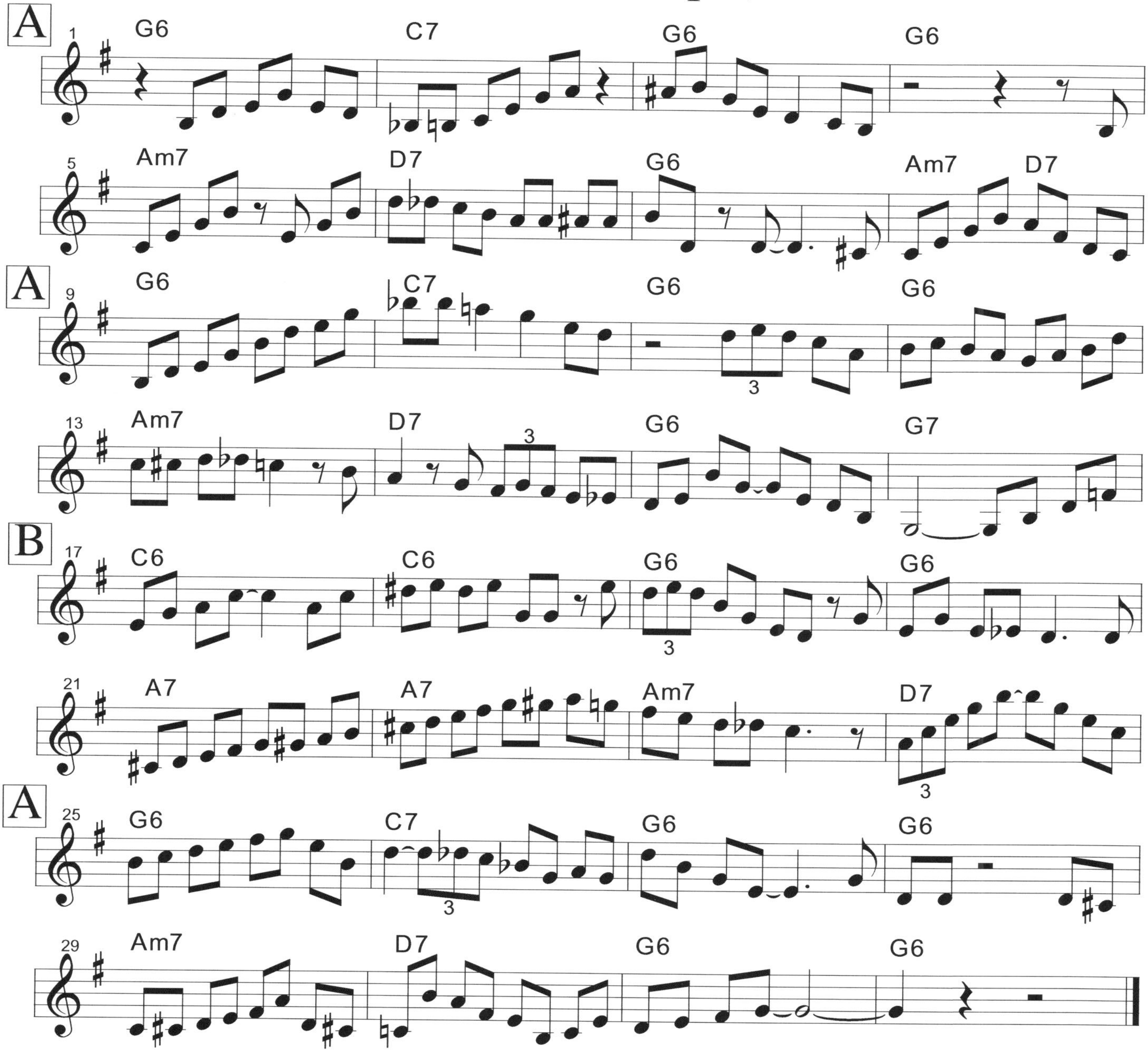

LESSON 16:
THE BEBOP SCALE IN G♭, B, E, AND A

THEORY:

We use the principles from lessons 4 and 5 to transpose the bebop scale to G♭, B, E, and A.

This lesson introduces the final four bebop scales G♭, B, E, and A. You should now know the bebop scale in all keys. As jazz players we strive to be fluent improvisers in all keys and should therefore practice the hard keys, like D♭, G♭, and B, even more than the easy ones. Please note the key of B can be played in half or first position on G and D but is always in first position on the A and E strings. Practice both!!! All the fingerings are designed to work with swing eighth and jazz bowings. Exercises 1-7 are basically the same as in lessons 5 and 10, but watch your fingerings carefully. As we saw earlier, the principle of the extra step of an ascending line being played with a finger sliding up and descending with a finger sliding down, is the same in most keys.

EXERCISES (CD tracks 4 and 5):

1.) **Play each scale starting on the root** all the way to the top in first position, then to the lowest note, then back up, etc. for eight measures. When using CD tracks 4 and 5 you may play the more advanced exercises including starts and stops in the easier keys. Then when the track goes into the new keys switch back to this simple exercise.

2.) **Play exercise 1 again using jazz slurs.** Samples are not written for exercises 2-4 or 6-7.

3.) **Play exercise 1 once more with a combination of single strokes and jazz slurs.**

4.) **Change direction.** Remember we still can not skip notes. Mix in jazz bowings.

5.) **Play the chord notes of the dominant 7 chord in all the keys.** Remember these are the regular four note dominant seventh chords we regard as chord notes when we use the bebop scale concept. Do not play the arpeggios from lesson 12. This exercise is merely a preparation exercise for exercises 6 and 7.

6.) **Start each phrase on a chord note on the beat**, then stop and start again.

7.) **Start each key on a non-chord note off the beat**, then stop and start again.

8.) **Add the voice leading notes from lesson 11.** In measure 8 of each key, play the 7th, then resolve it to the 3rd of the next chord. Repeat all the exercises from lesson 11 in the new keys.

Gb7   B7   E7   A7

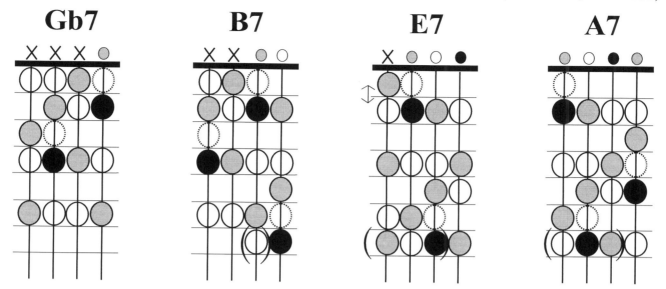

EXERCISES:

Exercise 1

Exercise 5

Exercise 8

LESSON 17:
THE CIRCLE OF FIFTHS

THEORY:

We use the inner melody from lesson 11 to navigate the circle of fifths.

In this lesson we still work with dominant bebop scales moving through all keys, with the exception that in this lesson track 11 only stays in each key for two measures. This provides a whole new set of challenges even though the basic theory is the same as in the previous lessons.

In example 1 we notice that if we play the ♭7 on every second chord and similarly the 3rd of every second chord we end up with a chromatically descending line.

When moving through multiple keys in this book we always go counter-clockwise on the circle of fifths. The circle of fifths (see example 2) is a common theoretical concept already covered in many music theory books. It is simply a way of organizing all major keys in fifths (or fourths counter-clockwise). It is helpful in identifying key signatures among other things. Please refer to the bibliography for more on the circle of fifths.

In our exercises all the keys become dominant seventh 5 chords. Our exercises start on D7 and go through the circle counter-clockwise. This way each key functions as the 5 chord to the next.

EXERCISES (CD track 11):

1.)   **Play the ♭7 to the 3rd of the next chord.** Then play the ♭7 of the following chord to the 3rd and so on. The line becomes a chromatic descending line.

2.)   Play strong **rhythmic melodies** incorporating the **inner melody line** (from Exercise 1).

3.)   Play simple **arpeggios** on each chord without using upper extensions.

4.)   Play simple **arpeggios** and combine them with the **inner melody line**.

5.)   Play **arpeggios** using **upper extensions**. Decide on a certain chord structure or shape and transpose it as seen in the sample exercises. Two great sounding structures are given. Sample 1 uses the 9, 3, 5, 7 shape. Sample 2 uses the 7, 3, 13, 1 shape. You can also use any of the 5 chord (D7) shapes from the examples in lesson 13.

6.)   Play simple **bebop scale** figures on each chord.

7.)   Play simple **bebop scale figures** and combine them with the **inner melody**. If you want to play all eighth notes you have to add an extra note (like an upper or lower neighbor note) between the ♭7 and 3 to keep following bebop scale rules.

8.)   **Combine all of the above.** You are now improvising while connecting all keys!

THEORY:

Example 1

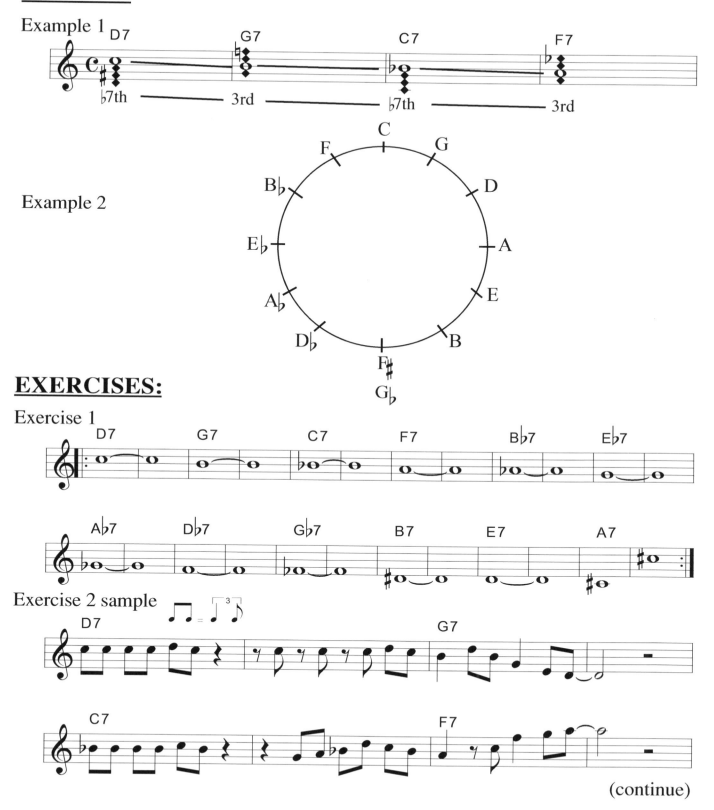

Example 2

EXERCISES:

Exercise 1

Exercise 2 sample

(continue)

Exercise 3 sample

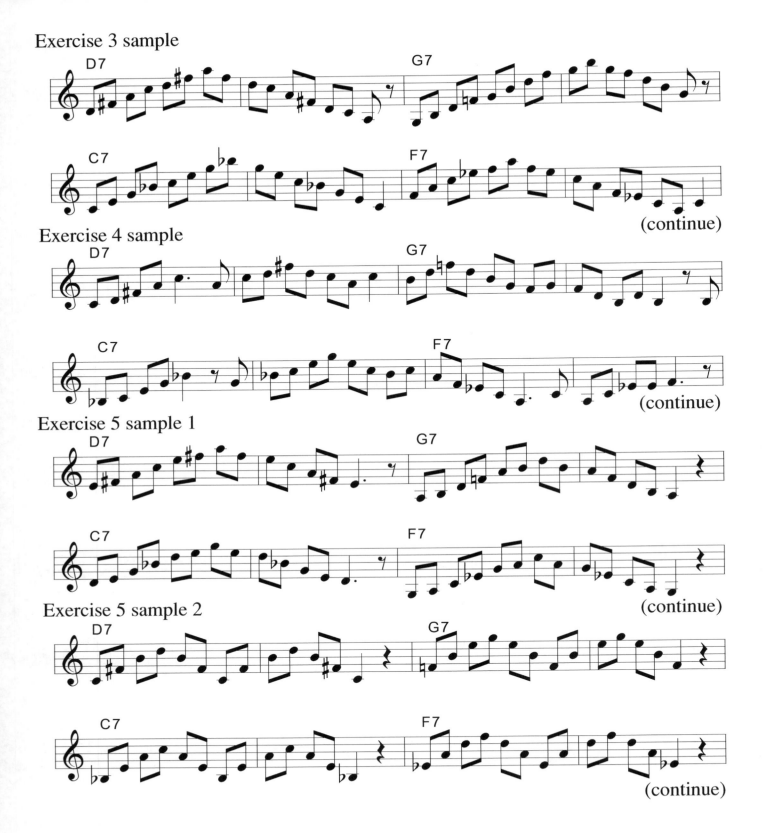

(continue)

Exercise 4 sample

(continue)

Exercise 5 sample 1

(continue)

Exercise 5 sample 2

(continue)

Exercise 6 sample

Exercise 7 sample

Exercise 8 sample

(continue)

LESSON 18:
THE 2m-5-1 IN ALL KEYS

THEORY:

We combine everything we know into one exercise.

This lesson basically combines lessons 12, 13, 14, and 16. In lessons 12-14 we learned different ways to approach playing on the most common progression in jazz, the 2m-5-1—arpeggios, regular scales, bebop scales, rhythms, and inner melodies. In lessons 12-14 we only played in G major. The following exercise takes the major 2m-5-1 through all keys. We start in the key of G, meaning the one chord is Gmaj7, the 2m is Am7, and the 5 is D7. Then we move to the key of C where the 2m is Dm7 and the 5 is G7, etc.

Practice the exercises to track 12 on the CD. Simply look at the key signature or the 1maj7 chord to determine what key you are in. Also refer to lessons 5, 10, and 16 to see the notes and fingerings for each bebop scale. For written examples of the following exercises simply transpose the samples in G major from lessons 12-14.

EXERCISES (CD track 12):

FROM LESSON 12:

1.) **Play the basic chords as arpeggios but without using upper extensions.**

2.) **Play the chords as arpeggios but in different inversions.**

3.) **Combine exercises 1 and 2 with a simple bebop scale lick.**

FROM LESSON 13:

1.) **Play arpeggios using arpeggio shapes.**

4.) **Combine arpeggio shapes, bebop scales and rhythms.**

FROM LESSON 14:

1.) **Play the basic scales of each chord ascending in eighth notes starting on the roots. Remember always to stay within the key of the 1 major 7 chord.**

2.) **Play the basic scales on the 2m and 1 but bebop on the 5 chord.**

3.) **Ignore the 2m and play the bebop scale of the 5 chord on the first two measures of each 2m-5-1.**

4.) **Add the inner melody (♭7-3) between the 5 and the 1 chords.**

5.) **Play arpeggios on the 2m, then go into the 5 bebop and use the inner melody to resolve to a great rhythm on the 1.**

6.) **MIX IT ALL UP AND MAKE IT YOUR OWN.**

EXERCISE:

(Lesson 18, continued)

This page has been left blank
to avoid awkward page turns.

TUNE DOWN

Up tempo

Martin Norgaard

Suggested listening: "Tune up," Stephane Grappelli - Stephanova

LESSON 19:
PHRASING AND *TUNE DOWN*

THEORY:

Good interesting phrasing means playing "over" the barline and away from boring four measure lines.

To play interesting solos, we not only have to play good notes and strong rhythms but also phrase well. The most common mistake is to always phrase following the chord pattern (like starting on the 2m and ending on the 1 on a 2m-5-1). This is of course exactly what we have done so far in all the 2m-5-1 exercises. But you should now be familiar enough with the basic scales and arpeggios to start experimenting with better phrasing.

As our example tune, I wrote a tune inspired by Miles Davis' classic *Tune Up*. *Tune Down* consists entirely of 2m-5-1's in D, C, and B♭ major. The tune may be practiced slow but should be performed up tempo.

All the exercises from the previous lesson apply but we are at the point where we should be able to cut loose and have fun improvising.

REMEMBER: WE THINK WHEN WE PRACTICE BUT NOT WHEN WE PERFORM. Try and imagine you are performing while playing *Tune Down* to track 13.

The solo example is just one way of experimenting with the phrasing. The figure in measure 1 ends in measure 3. The lick starting in measure 4 ends in measure 6. Then a long line goes all the way from measure 7 to 12 with a small space in measure 9. Only measures 13 to 16 are within the four measure phrase of the 2m-5-1's, though this line helps to resolve the faster line before it.

The solo example has chromatic passing tones in measures 1 (C), 8 (A♭), and 12 (A♭, F♯). It uses arpeggios in measures 1, 7, 11, and 15 and rhythms in measures 4, 5, 6, 11, and 13-16. The bebop scale is used in measures 9 and 10 and the ♭7 to 3 inner melody is implied in measures 1-2 and 2-3. The rhythmic figure in measures 5 and 6 implies an inner melody we have not yet analyzed (C♯-C-B). More on that later.

EXERCISES (CD track 13):

1.) **Play various arpeggios on all the chords.** See lessons 12 and 13.

2.) **Play scales on all chords.** See lesson 14.

3.) **Mix up scales and arpeggios with interesting rhythms.**

4.) **Play a longer solo over many choruses and experiment with phrases that connect the 2m-5-1's.** This is done by starting a lick in measure 3 and ending in measure 5, etc., thereby phrasing away from the four bar phrases outlined by the chords.

TUNE DOWN
(chord analysis)

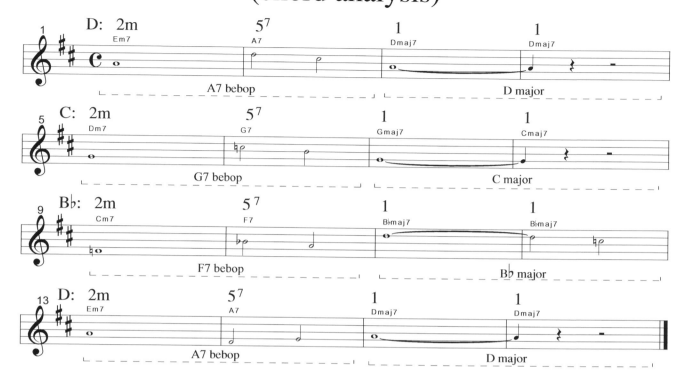

Solo example

LESSON 20:
ALTERING THE 5, PART 1

THEORY:

By sharping the 5th of the dominant seventh chord we add new possibilities for interesting arpeggios and inner melodies.

So far we have not altered any notes within the chords. Even though we learned in lesson 12 that the 9th, 11th, and 13th are implied as part of the dominant 7th chord, those extensions were still diatonic. That means the upper extensions are still part of the regular mixolydian scale. In other words, in the key of G, all the notes of the D13 are still part of D mixolydian, which has the same notes as G major.

In this lesson we will introduce a non-diatonic chord tone to the 5 chord. This may not sound like much but it opens up a whole new world of possibilities. In example 1, we see the regular D7 with the implied upper extensions marked in squares. Next to it is the D7$^{(\sharp 5)}$, also referred to as D7aug. The 11th and 13th extensions are not listed because they are usually very hard to use when combined with a sharped 5th.

Example 2 shows the chords of a 2m-5-1 in G where the D7 is altered to a D7$^{(\sharp 5)}$. The lines show examples of inner melodies utilizing the augmented 5th. Inner melody 1 uses the root of Am7 (A) to $\sharp$5 of D7 (A$\sharp$) to the 3rd of Gmaj7 (B). Inner melody 2 uses the 9th of Am7 (B) to $\sharp$5 of D7 (A$\sharp$) to the 9th of Gmaj7 (A). Though these two chromatic inner melody lines look similar they actually function quite differently because one uses upper extensions while the other one doesn't.

Please note that even when a jazz chord chart only lists the 5 chord as a regular dominant 7th we can alter the 5 chord, as long as the 5 resolves to 1. Therefore we can practice this to both track 9 (2m-5-1's in G) and track 12 (2m-5-1's in all keys).

EXERCISES (CD tracks 9 and 12):

1.)   **Play the two inner melodies in example 2 repeatedly to track 9.**

2.)   **Transpose the two inner melodies to all keys using track 12.**

3.)   **Improvise combining inner melody 1 (1-$\sharp$5-3) with arpeggios.** Again, first use track 9 and practice in G only (see sample). Then transpose to all keys using track 12.

4.)   **Improvise combining inner melody 2 (9-$\sharp$5-9) with arpeggios.** Use tracks 9 and 12.

5.)   **Improvise combining inner melody 1 (1-$\sharp$5-3) with bebop scale licks.**

6.)   **Improvise using the #5 on the D7 without an apparent inner melody.**

7.)   **Combine rhythms with all of the above.**

THEORY:

EXERCISES:

Exercise 3 sample

Exercise 4 sample

Exercise 5 sample

Exercise 6 sample

Exercise 7 sample

LESSON 21:
ALTERING THE 5, PART 2

THEORY:

By sharping and flatting the 9th of the dominant seventh chord we add new opportunities for great sounding licks with new arpeggios and inner melodies.

Altering the 9th of the 5 chord opens up even more possibilities. It works with either a flatted or sharped 9th. But most remarkably it works both flatted and sharped simultaneously. Example 1 shows the D7, D7$^{(\flat 9)}$, D7$^{(\sharp 9)}$, and the D7$^{(\flat 9\sharp 9)}$ chords. Notice the $\sharp$9 (E$\sharp$) can be spelled as a minor 3rd (F$\natural$). This spelling accentuates the fact that the $\sharp$9 is the same note as the minor third, leaving us with a chord that contains both a minor and a major 3rd. Try to play the chords on a piano—it sounds great. As with the sharp 5th alteration from lesson 20, the two 9th alterations work on nearly all 5 chords as long as they resolve to 1 even if it is listed in the chart as being a regular dominant 7th.

Example 2 shows four inner melodies that we will now turn into very cool licks.

EXERCISES (CD tracks 9 and 12):

1.) **Play inner melody 1 (5-$\flat$9-5) first in G using track 9, then in all keys, using track 12:** a) Just in whole notes; b) Adding a great rhythm and simple melody; c) Combined with scales; d) Combined with arpeggios; e) Combined with a combination of rhythms, scales and arpeggios.

2.) **Play inner melody 2 (9-$\flat$9-5) first in G, then in all keys:** a) in whole notes; b) with rhythms; c) with scales; d) with arpeggios; e) all of the above.

3.) **Play inner melody 3 (7-$\sharp$9-$\flat$9-5) first in G, then in all keys:** a) in whole notes; b) with rhythms; c) with scales; d) with arpeggios; e) all of the above.

4.) **Play inner melody 4 (5-$\sharp$9-7) first in G, then in all keys:** a) in whole notes; b) with rhythms; c) with scales; d) with arpeggios; e) all of the above.

5.) **Combine the $\flat$9 and $\sharp$9 with the $\sharp$5. Use no apparent inner melody.** If you have done the exercises above for a while you should be able to improvise with the alterations without thinking. I took a lot of liberties creating these samples. They include chromatic passing tones and integrate a couple of advanced techniques (like implied triads and fourths).

THEORY:

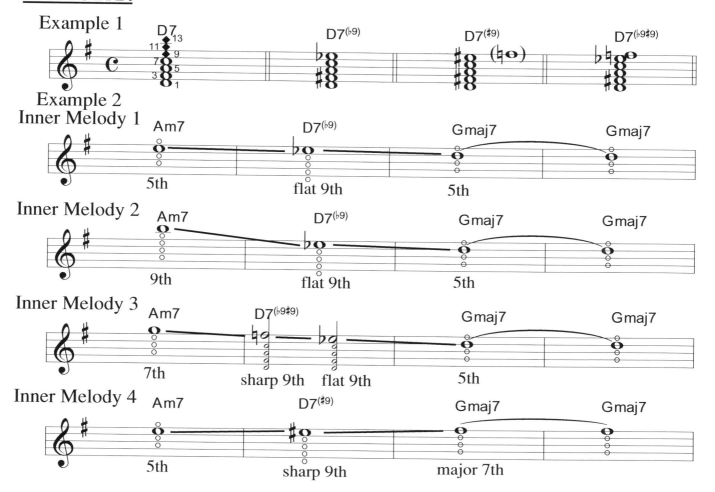

Example 1

Example 2
Inner Melody 1

Inner Melody 2

Inner Melody 3

Inner Melody 4

WARNING: DO NOT BECOME AN EXPERT IN JUST G MAJOR BY NEVER TRANSPOSING THE FOLLOWING EXERCISES. Jazz moves through all keys. Even though it seems like tedious work you must transpose the following exercises to all keys. The best way is by working on a couple of keys per practice similar to the way this book introduced the bebop scale. Try to transpose by ear. Start with the easy inner melody lines. Then improvise using the inner melody lines as starting points and the licks on the following pages as samples. When you are ready, play a particular lick or concept in all keys using track 12.

EXERCISES:

Exercise 1b sample

Exercise 1c sample

Exercise 3e sample

Exercise 4b sample

Exercise 4c sample

Exercise 4d sample

Exercise 4e sample

Exercise 5 samples

LESSON 22:
THE MINOR 2°-5-1m

THEORY:

The minor 2°-5-1m uses the diatonic chords and scales on the 1st, 2nd, and 5th step of the 1m's natural (or aeolian) minor scale.

The minor 2°-5-1m is a common building block in jazz and it is important to be able to improvise on the minor 2°-5-1m of any key. Just like on the major 2m-5-1 where we basically played in the key of the major scale on all three chords, we can play the natural minor scale of the 1m on all the chords of the 2°-5-1m.

In this lesson we are still in G major, as we were when we introduced the major 2m-5-1 in lessons 12 to 14. The only difference is that we count everything starting from the relative minor of G major which is E minor. Example 1 lists both set of numbers where the 1 is determined by whether we count from G as in G major or E as in E minor.

In example 2 each of the chords of the minor 2°-5-1m is listed. The first chord is a F#m7$^{(b5)}$. We refer to the minor 7th ♭5 chord as a half diminished and write the chord as $^°$. The scale that fits the chord is referred to as the locrian scale, as seen in the first measure of example 3. The locrian scale is a regular major scale starting on the seventh step or a natural minor starting on the second step. The F# locrian scale contains the same notes as G major. To bring out the sound of the F# locrian we emphasize the chord notes F#, A, C, and E. Notice that on the F#$^°$ we avoid upper extensions.

The second chord in example 2 is a B7$^{(b9#9)}$. We learned in lesson 21 that most 5 chords work with the 9th being altered. In most minor 2°-5-1m's the 5 chord is listed with some kind of alteration. By using the scale on the fifth step of the natural minor (referred to as the phrygian minor scale) and at times adding a major third (referred to as a Spanish phrygian), we end up with a scale that fits the B7$^{(b9#9)}$ (see measure 2 in example 3). We accentuate the basic chord by emphasizing the chord notes of the B7 without the upper extensions (B, D#, F#, and A). Notice our B7$^{(b9#9)}$ scale also has a flat 13th (G).

The third chord in example 2 is a regular minor 7th chord. If we stay in the key of G we end up playing an E natural minor scale, also referred to as an aeolian minor (see measure 3 in example 3). We can however also use a dorian minor on the 1m.

This lesson outlines the simplest way to play on a minor 2°-5-1m. Play the following exercises to track 14 on the CD that simply repeats a minor 2°-5-1m in E minor.

EXERCISES (CD track 14):

1.) **Play on the minor 2°-5-1m in Em repeatedly using only the E natural minor scale:**

a) using scales only; b) using arpeggios mixed with scales (use D# only as part of a B7$^{(b9#9)}$ arpeggio).

2.) **Repeat exercise 1 but add the D# to the scale on the 5 chord, B7$^{(b9#9)}$:**

a) using scales only; b) using arpeggios mixed with scales.

THEORY:

Example 1

E minor scale step numbers: 1 2 3 4 5 6 7 1 2 3
G major step numbers: 6 7 1 2 3 4 5 6 7 1

Example 2

F#ø (or F#m7♭5)   B7(♭9♯9)   Em7

2ø   5   1m

Example 3

F#ø   B7(♭9♯9)   Em7

F# locrian   B phrygian plus D#   E natural minor

EXERCISES:

Exercise 1a sample

F#ø   B7(♭9♯9)   Em7   Em7

Exercise 1b sample

F#ø   B7(♭9♯9)   Em7   Em7

Exercise 2a sample

F#ø   B7(♭9♯9)   Em7   Em7

Exercise 2b sample

F#ø   B7(♭9♯9)   Em7   Em7

75

LESSON 23:
THE MINOR 2ø-5-1m IN ALL KEYS

THEORY:

We transpose the scales and licks from lesson 22 and combine them with a couple of techniques we learned studying the major 2m-5-1.

This lesson combines lesson 22 with a couple of concepts learned earlier in the book. These include rhythms and arpeggios.

The following exercises go through all minor keys using track 15 on the CD. We start in the key of E minor, meaning the one chord is Em, the $2^{ø}$ is F$\sharp^{ø}$ (or F$\sharp$m$7^{(b5)}$), and the 5 is B$7^{(b9\sharp9)}$. Then we move to the key of A minor where the $2^{ø}$ is B^{ø} and the 5 is E$7^{(b9\sharp9)}$, etc. Notice that the minor keys are arranged around the circle of fifths just like the 2m-5-1 exercise in lesson 18. That means we add or take away one sharp or flat going from line to line – e.g., line 1 is in E minor or G major and has one sharp. Line 2 is in A minor or C major and has no accidentals. Line 3 is in D minor or F major and has one flat, etc.

To help determine what key to use for improvising, the key signature is listed for each line. Also remember the minor key's relative major scale is always a half step above the root of the first chord of each $2^{ø}$-5-1m. For written examples of the following exercises simply transpose the samples in E minor from lesson 22 to each key.

EXERCISES (CD track 15):

1.) **Play on all the minor $2^{ø}$-5-1m's using only the natural minor scale of each key**. Start the lick on the root of the $2^{ø}$ and go up and down the scale without too many skips. As we saw in lesson 22, one basic scale fits over all three chords of the minor $2^{ø}$-5-1m. See exercise 1a sample in lesson 22 for a written example of this exercise.

2.) **Play on all the minor $2^{ø}$-5-1m's using only the natural minor scale of each key**. This time start on a note other than the root of the $2^{ø}$ chord.

3.) **Arpeggiate each chord of all the minor $2^{ø}$-5-1m's**. Transpose each of the basic chords (no upper extensions) from example 2 in lesson 22 and arpeggiate those through all keys.

4.) **Use a combination of the natural minor scale and arpeggios** to improvise over all the minor $2^{ø}$-5-1m's. See exercise 1b sample in lesson 22.

5.) **Add the 5 chords major third to the scale on the 5 chord**. Use mainly scales. See exercise 2a sample from lesson 22.

6.) **Repeat exercise 5 but add arpeggios**. See exercise 2b sample from lesson 22.

EXERCISE:

(Lesson 23, continued)

This page has been left blank
to avoid awkward page turns.

YOU CAN'T APPEAR AGAIN

Medium

Martin Norgaard

Suggested listening: "There Will Never Be Another You," Svend Asmussen - Fiddler Supreme

LESSON 24:

PASSING CHORDS AND *YOU CAN'T...*

THEORY:

We can choose not to improvise over passing chords. When improvising on *You Can't Appear Again* we use major and minor 2-5-1 licks, bebop scales, and rhythms.

We can use everything we have learned so far when improvising over *You Can't Appear Again*, an original tune built roughly on the same chords as the classic standard *There Will Never Be Another You*.

The scales listed in the chord analysis are the most basic. The first line starts in the key of E♭ major, then modulates to the relative minor through a minor 2ø-5-1m in C minor. We discovered in lesson 22 that we can get away with playing the E♭ major scale over the minor 2ø-5-1m because it is going to the relative minor of E♭ major, C minor. Of course we would like to apply some of the principles and licks from lesson 22 that outline all the chords of the minor 2ø-5-1m. In measure 7 we start analyzing from A♭ because the 2m-5-1 leading to A♭ clearly shows that the tune modulates. In measure 10 the D♭7 is the 4 of A♭ but I chose to analyze the chord from E♭ because the following chords bring us back to E♭ major; therefore it becomes a ♭7⁷ chord. Measure 28 has a dominant chord on the 7th step of E♭ major. Though a dominant chord on either the flat seven or major seventh step can be explained, remember that the tune came first and the analysis afterwards.

The last line contains a number of 7th chords mainly going through the circle of fifths back to the one. When improvising we can easily get away with simply ignoring the chords and staying in E♭ major. We often refer to fast moving chords that don't signal a modulation as passing chords.

EXERCISES (CD track 16):

1.) **Play simple arpeggios starting on the roots of the chords.** See lessons 12 and 13. Be sure to always keep your place. Try to memorize the chords. Use track 16 on the CD.

2.) **Improvise using the scales listed in the chord analysis.**

3.) **Insert your favorite licks.** Start using some of the concepts introduced in the later lessons by transposing and inserting the sample licks in the tune. See written sample.

4.) **Improvise adding one of the concepts the licks from exercise 3 represent** – e.g., the lick in measures 7-9 from lesson 13 uses an arpeggio shape. Try to improvise over the whole tune using as many of that particular arpeggio shape as possible in addition to the regular scales. You can also try to augment the 5th of all the 5 chords as we did in lesson 20.

5.) **Improvise using multiple licks and concepts.** See written solo example.

YOU CAN'T APPEAR AGAIN
(chord analysis)

Martin Norgaard

Exercise 3 sample

Exercise 1b sample from lesson 22

Exercise 1 sample from lesson 13

Exercise 3d sample from lesson 21

Exercise 2b sample from lesson 22

Beginning of Exercise 6 sample from lesson 7

YOU CAN'T APPEAR AGAIN
(solo example)

This page has been left blank
to avoid awkward page turns.

INDIANA (BACK HOME AGAIN IN)

McDonald/Hanley
arr. M. Norgaard

Suggested listening: The Fabulous Joe Venuti: 15 Jazz Classics

LESSON 25:

PLAYING FAST AND *INDIANA*

THEORY:

The key to playing fast is by thinking and feeling in cut time.

Indiana is very similar to *You Can't Appear Again*. As shown in the analysis on the next page the tune starts in A♭ and goes by way of a ♭7 passing chord to the 6 and 2 back to a 2m-5-1 in A♭. Just as in *You Can't Appear Again* the tune modulates to the 4 of A♭, D♭, by the way of a 2m-5-1 in D♭. Through a ♭7^7 it modulates back to A♭. The second half modulates to the relative minor of A♭, F minor, through a minor 2$^\emptyset$-5-1m. Of course, as we saw in lesson 22, we can still use the notes of A♭ major through the 2$^\emptyset$-5-1m to F minor. Measures 1, 17, 29, and 30 contain fast moving passing chords that we can choose to ignore, including the B diminished chord in measure 29. In measure 28 we can either ignore the F diminished or play over an F^0 arpeggio (F, A♭, B, D).

The main challenge we face improvising over *Indiana* is that the tune is generally played in a very fast tempo. We approach faster tempos by thinking in cut time. That means we imagine there are only two beats per measure. Instead of eighth notes, our improvised solo will consist mostly of sixteenth notes. The exercises in this lesson should each be done three different ways: a) improvise to the slower version on the practice CD (track 17) using mostly eighth notes; b) improvise to the slower version but use mainly sixteenth notes, also referred to as double time (this means you suddenly have to come up with twice as many notes as before because every chord lasts twice as long); c) play to the fast track which is exactly twice as fast as the slower track. Go back to the licks you used in exercise a, but duplicate the feel and phrasing of your licks in exercise b. Tap your foot on beat 1 and 3 and relax even though you are playing fast.

EXERCISES (CD tracks 17 and 18):

1.) **Play scales ascending on each chord starting on the root**: a) in eighth notes to track 17; b) in sixteenth notes to track 17; c) in eighth notes to track 18. Only the beginning of each exercise is written out. Continue playing the same exercise until the end of the track. Also try this in easier keys by applying these principles to tunes from previous lessons.

2.) **Play scales but change direction without starting on the roots**: a) in eighth notes to track 17; b) in sixteenth notes to track 17; c) in eighth notes to track 18. Add rests to follow the bebop scale rules on all the dominant seven chords.

3.) **Insert your favorite licks**: a) in eighth notes to track 17; b) in sixteenth notes to track 17. You have to start the lick later because it is only half as long. On the 2m-5-1 licks the resolve to 1 should correspond to the chords; c) in eighth notes to track 18.

4.) **Improvise with the concepts the licks from exercise 3 represent**. Improvise both to track 17 and 18. See solo example.

INDIANA (BACK HOME AGAIN IN)
(chord analysis)

Exercise 1a & 1c

Exercise 1b

Exercise 2a & 2c sample

Exercise 2b sample

Exercise 3a & 3c sample

Beginning of Exercise 5 sample 1 from lesson 17

Exercise 4 sample from lesson 20

(continue)

88

Exercise 3b sample

(continue)

INDIANA (BACK HOME AGAIN IN)
(solo example)

BIBLIOGRAPHY

The following is a list of resources that cover some of the things not taught in *Jazz Fiddle Wizard*. Notice that except for using Stuff Smith to set an example for jazz rhythms I have not included any lessons on style and sound. It is my firm belief that jazz violin can be played as many different ways as there are players. Stephane Grappelli played with a sweet sound similar to classical phrasing. Stuff Smith played and phrased much like his hero, trumpet player Louis Armstrong. A number of great players including Buddy Spicher and Johnny Gimble play jazz tunes with a strong western swing flavor.

It is my experience that not mixing the study of styles with the study of improvising facilitates the player finding his or her own sound. First, study improvising without insisting on specific stylistic elements like slides or a dry tone. Then study transcriptions of some of the great jazz violin stylists. Without fail some of the stylistic elements from the transcription will become part of the player's improvising. The book *Jazz Violin*, by Matt Glaser and Stephane Grappelli, is a great resource for transcriptions and style analysis. One can learn much by imitating the great players and learning their solos note for note off a recording, as long as one doesn't emulate one player exclusively and as long as one realizes that this study alone will not teach one how to improvise.

When it comes to learning tunes, the huge series of music minus one recordings by Jamey Aebersold is an invaluable tool.

For studying the history of the violin in jazz, I recommend Anthony Barnett's marvelous book on Stuff Smith, *Desert Sands*, and his Fable Bulletin: *Violin Improvisation Studies*.

For comparison between jazz and classical theory, try researching various concepts like the cadence or the circle of fifths in Robert Ottman's book, *Elementary Harmony*.

For further studies in jazz theory specifically aimed at strings, I suggest David Baker's book.

For a different angle on improvising including a wider range of styles and information about the physical aspects of violin playing, try Julie Lyonn Lieberman's books.

The following list of the books is by no means complete. I highly recommend checking my web site **http://www.jazzfiddlewizard.com** for more up to date information and resources.

Books:

Baker, David N. *Jazz Expressions and Explorations for Strings.* New Albany, IN: Jamey Aebersold Jazz, Inc., 1995.

Barnett, Anthony. *Desert Sands. Vol. 1.* East Sussex, Eng.: Allardyce, Barnett, Publishers, 1995 and supplement: *Up Jumped the Devil.* 1998.

Barnett, Anthony. *Fable Bulletin: Violin Improvisation Studies.* 11 vols. to date. East Sussex, Eng.: Allardyce, Barnett, Publishers, 1993-99.

Blake, John, and Jody Harmon. *Jazz Improvisation Made Easy.* Westford, MA: JIME, 1993.

Glaser, Matt, and Stephane Grappelli. *Jazz Violin.* New York: Oak Publications, 1981.

Lieberman, Julie Lyonn. *Improvising Violin.* New York: Huiksi Music, 1995.

Ottman, Robert W. *Elementary Harmony: Theory and Practice.* 5th ed. Upper Saddle River, NJ : Prentice-Hall, 1997.

Play-a-long CDs:

Aebersold, Jamey. *A New Approach to Jazz Improvisation.* 77 vols. to date. New Albany, IN : Jamey Aebersold Jazz, Inc., 1974- .

Websites:

(due to the changing nature of the web make sure to check **jazzfiddlewizard.com** for updated information)

http://www.jazzfiddlewizard.com/
(The official web site by the author of this book)

http://shoko.calarts.edu/~chung/JazzViolin.html
(Thanks to Mark Chung for a great web site with tons of information and great links. Also thanks to John Reeves for putting audio samples from his extensive collection on the web)

http://clubs.yahoo.com/clubs/alternativestrings
(A discussion site started by Mark Chung)

http://www.lightbubble.com/bowed/index.html
(Guide to amplification and players in many styles)

http://www.geocities.com/~jimlowe/svend/svendex.html
(Great site about Svend Asmussen)

DISCOGRAPHY

Probably the most important thing in learning to improvise within the jazz tradition is listening. This should include listening to all the jazz greats. Specifically listening to great jazz violinists is both comforting and challenging. Comforting, because it proves that you are not alone and that the violin is a great jazz instrument. Challenging, because the recordings set a standard by which all new players will be judged.

Here is a very selective collection of some of my favorite recordings. Only the listed LPs and a couple of foreign import CDs are really hard to find (marked with *). The rest should be available in larger record stores, like Jazz Record Mart in Chicago (www.jazzmart.com), or on the web. The recordings are listed chronologically for each artist. This discography mainly contains classic recordings. Check **jazzfiddlewizard.com** for an updated list of CDs with more contemporary improvising string players. **Jazzfiddlewizard.com** also contains a link to my online radio station which plays classic jazz violin recordings.

Svend Asmussen:

Asmussen, Svend. *Svend Asmussen Musical Miracle Vol. 1: 1935-40*. Phontastic, PHONT CD 9306, 1994.

Asmussen, Svend. *Svend Asmussen Phenomenal Fiddler Vol. 2: 1941-50*. Phontastic, PHONT CD 9310, 1995.

Asmussen, Svend, and Stephane Grappelli. *Two of a Kind*. Rec. 23 & 24 Jan. 1965. Storyville, STCD 4088, 1986.

Asmussen, Svend, Svend Asmussen Quartet. *Fiddler Supreme*. Rec. June 1989. Intim Musik, IMCD 006, 1989.

Stephane Grappelli:

(earlier recordings use the spelling Grappelly)

Reinhardt, Django, and Stephane Grappelli. *Django Reinhardt & Stephane Grappelli*. Rec. 1934-40 (?). Pearl Flapper 9738, 1993.

Grappelly, Stephane. *Stephane Grappelly 1935-1940*. Classics 708, 1993.

Grappelly, Stephane, and Django Reinhardt with The Quintet of the Hot Club of France. *Souvenirs*. Rec. 1938-46. London 820 591-2, 1988.

Grappelli, Stephane. *Parisian Thoroughfare*. Rec. 5 & 7 Sep. 1973. Black Lion, BLCD760132, 1989.

Grappelli, Stephane. *Stephanova*. Rec. June 1983. Concord Jazz, CCD-4225, 1989.

Jean-Luc Ponty:

Ponty, Jean-Luc. *Sunday Walk*. Rec. June 1967. LP. MPS 20645, 1972.*

Ponty, Jean-Luc, and Stephane Grappelli. *Compact Jazz*. PDG/Verve, 35320, 1988.

(This CD includes 3 cuts from *Sunday Walk*)

Ponty, Jean-Luc, Eddy Louiss and Daniel Humair. *Humair-Louiss-Ponty*. Rec. 1968. Dreyfus Jazz, FDM 36515-2, 1997.

Ponty, Jean-Luc. *More Than Meets the Ear*. Rec. 1969. One Way Records 17605, 1994.

Ponty, Jean-Luc. *Live at Donte's*. Rec. 12 & 13 March 1969. Pacific Jazz CDP 7243 8 35635 2 4, 1995.

Ponty, Jean-Luc, Al Di Meola and Stanley Clarke. *The Rite of Strings*. Rec. April 1995. Gai Saber 7243 8 34167 2 1, 1995.

Zbigniew Seifert:

Seifert, Zbigniew. *Man of the Light*. Rec. 27-30 Sept. 1976. LP. Pausa 7077, 1980.*

Seifert, Zbigniew. *Passion*. Rec. Nov. 1978. LP. Capitol Records, ST-11923, 1979.*

Stuff Smith:

Smith, Stuff. *Stuff Smith and His Onyx Club Boys* 1936-1939. Classics 706, 1993.

Smith, Stuff. *Stuff Smith 1939-1944*. Classics 1054, 1999.

Smith, Stuff. *Onyx Club Spree*. Rec. 1936-1945. Topaz Jazz, TPZ 1061, 1997.

Smith, Stuff. *The Stuff Smith Trio-1943*. Progressive, PCD-7053, 1988.

Smith, Stuff, Dizzy Gillespie and Oscar Peterson. *Stuff Smith-Dizzy Gillespie-Oscar Peterson*. Rec. 1957. Verve 314 521 676-2, 1994.

Smith, Stuff. *The Complete Verve Stuff Smith Sessions*. Rec. 1956-1964. Mosaic, M04 - 186, 1999.

Ellis, Herb and Stuff Smith. *Together!* Rec. 8 Jan. 1963. Koch Jazz, Koc 3-7805-2, 1995.

Smith, Stuff. *Live at the Montmartre*. Rec. 18 March 1965. Storyville STCD 4142, 1988.

Eddie South:

South, Eddie. *Eddie South 1923-1937*. Classics 707, 1992.

Turtle Island String Quartet:

Turtle Island String Quartet. *A Windham Hill Retrospective*. Windham Hill, 01934-11226-2, 1997.

Michal Urbaniak:

Urbaniak, Michal. *Fusion*. Rec. 1974. Sony Music, 65525, 1998.

Joe Venuti:

Venuti, Joe. *Violin Jazz 1927 to 1934*. Yazoo 1062, 1989.

Venuti, Joe, and George Barnes. *Gems*. Rec. Aug. 1975. Concord Jazz, CCD-6014, 1994.

Venuti, Joe. *The Fabulous Joe Venuti: 15 Jazz Classics*. Rec. 1971 & 1974. Omega, OCD 3019, 1995.

Various Artists:

Various Artists, Stuff Smith, Stephane Grappelli, Svend Asmussen and Jean-Luc Ponty. *Violin Summit*. Rec. 30 Sept. 1966. MPS 821 303-2, n.d.*

.

Made in the USA
San Bernardino, CA
16 August 2016